ALL THAT GOD
HAS GIVEN

HARTLAND H. GIFFORD

ALL THAT GOD HAS GIVEN

FAITHFUL STEWARDSHIP AS FOLLOWERS OF JESUS

Augsburg

MINNEAPOLIS

ALL THAT GOD HAS GIVEN
Faithful Stewardship as Followers of Jesus

Scripture quotations are from the New Revised Standard Version Bible, copyright ©
1989 by the Division of Christian Education of the National Council of the Churches
of Christ in the United States of America. Used with permission.

Text of "A Mighty Fortress Is Our God" is copyright © 1978 *Lutheran Book of Worship*.

Cover and interior design: James F. Brisson

Library of Congress Cataloging-in-Publication Data

Gifford, Hartland H.
    All that God has given : faithful stewardship as followers of
Jesus / Hartland H. Gifford.
        p.   cm.
    ISBN 0-8066-2655-0 :
    1. Stewardship, Christian.   I. Title.
    BV772.G48   1993
    248'.6—dc20   92-31987
                                                                       CIP

The paper used in this publication meets the minimum requirements of American
National Standard for Information Sciences—Permanence of paper for Printed Library
Materials, ANSI Z329.48-1984.   ∞™

Manufactured in the U.S.A.   AF 9-2655

97   96   95   94   93   1   2   3   4   5   6   7   8   9   10

CONTENTS

PREFACE

More often than not, stewardship is regarded as a program of the church—that is done to support a congregation's budget. This limited view is unfortunate because stewardship encompasses much more. It is our personal response to the call of Jesus Christ to be faithful stewards of all God's gifts. Thus, stewardship relates to the totality of life. It is our management of what God has entrusted to us.

Stewardship is not just the money we give, nor is it a few hours donated to the church or some worthy cause. It is more than using our abilities to help others when we have some free time. Rather, stewardship is what we do with all that God has given us—our very lives, our every breath, all of our possessions, every ability—100 percent of the time. What we do on Tuesday morning and Thursday evening is as much a part of our stewardship as what we do on Sunday morning.

This book is an attempt to view stewardship in the light of the life, ministry, death, and resurrection of Jesus, the Christ. As such, it is a study of *Christian* stewardship.

The center of Christian theology is the cross of Christ, but unless we know something about Jesus' life, how can we attach any meaning to his death? This study approaches our Lord's life in some detail, more or less chronologically (as presented in the Gospels), beginning with his baptism and continuing to his ascension.

Biblical scholars tell us that it is not possible to write a biography of Jesus from the information given in the Gospels. There is, however, a pattern in what we know of his life that can inform our understanding of stewardship. The various recorded events fit together; there is a relationship, for example, between the temptations and the feeding of the five thousand. There is a relationship between the transfiguration and the ascension. The teaching of Jesus is filled with stewardship issues, and has a bearing on how we can live our lives as faithful stewards. In Jesus' life we find a model for our response (stewardship).

As far as we know, Jesus never referred to himself as a steward. He used such phrases as "The Good Shepherd" or "Son of Man" to describe his role. The latter seems to have been his favorite. It was the equivalent of "a man," it was well known by his listeners. It had been used for centuries, but approximately 70 B.C., a Jewish writing called Enoch used the term "Son of Man" to describe a superhuman being who would come with the full authority of God to be victorious over the enemies of God. So when Jesus referred to himself as the Son of Man, his hearers knew that he was claiming to be from God. However, their notion of who was coming and what he would do was very different from that of Jesus.

The professional religionists were often incensed by the words and actions of Jesus. He didn't say and do what they thought a religious teacher should say and do. He ate with sinners. He broke laws on the Sabbath. He put a new light on things they had been taught. They thought that he was more in league with the devil than with God. Not only did this cause anger and resentment on their part, it often caused confusion and questioning. Even the disciples of Jesus at times would puzzle over the question, "Who is this?"

From our perspective, however, we believe that Jesus lived a life in total obedience to God's will. If ever there was a faithful steward it was Jesus. Indeed, Jesus is the best example we have of what it means to be totally dedicated to God.

Ultimately, Jesus passed his ministry on to his disciples. Today that ministry is our ministry. We are called by our Lord to manage all that has been given to us by God.

In the following chapters we will suggest what this can mean in our own lives. No book can outline fully what it means to be a good steward. We can only learn that as we give ourselves to God, seeking to know and do God's will in our lives.

1
THE BAPTISM
OF JESUS

Called to ministry

Jesus was approximately thirty years old when he came to the Jordan River to be baptized by his cousin John. All four gospels tell the story. It was a time of religious revival. Great numbers of people were coming to John, a strange prophet, to hear his preaching and to be baptized.

From Mark we learn that John "appeared in the wilderness, proclaiming a baptism of repentance for the forgiveness of sins" (MARK 1:4) and that he "was clothed with camel's hair, with a leather belt around his waist, and he ate locusts and wild honey" (MARK 1:6). "People from the whole Judean countryside and all the people of Jerusalem were going out to him, and were baptized by him in the river Jordan, confessing their sins" (MARK 1:5). In many respects this was so unusual that it might defy explanation. For centuries the Jews had thought of themselves as God's chosen people. Baptism was a ritual cleansing for those who wanted to become Jews, but the chosen of God thought they had no need of such washing. Yet the crowds kept coming, and Jesus came with them.

Baptism as witness

From our vantage point we ask why Jesus needed to confess his sins and be baptized. John may well have felt the same way. His immediate reaction was to refuse to baptize Jesus. "I need to be baptized by you," he told Jesus, "and do you come to me?" (MATTHEW 3:14). But Jesus insisted. "Let it be so now," he said to John, "for it is proper for us in this way to fulfill all righteousness" (MATTHEW 3:15).

The baptism of Jesus was intended as a witness. Jesus was saying, in effect, "This is the appointed time. A new age is dawning. I am taking my place with those who seek God, seeking to do God's will." And, of course, that was a hallmark of his entire life. For us it is a powerful lesson, teaching us that to respond to God's call is to seek God's will in all things.

So it is that John consented to baptize Jesus. But a curious thing happened. As Jesus emerged from the water, the heavens opened (says Matthew) and Jesus saw the Spirit of God descending like a dove, and heard a voice from heaven: "This is my Son, the Beloved, with whom I am well pleased" (MATTHEW 3:17). This is a phrase we will hear again. Keep it in mind, for it has an important bearing on our study.

The benefits of baptism

Just as the baptism of Jesus marked the start of his ministry, so does our part in the family of the church begin with our baptism. Baptism begins our life of faith. It is a one-time event that lasts a lifetime.

In baptism we are freed from the power of sin and death. Martin Luther ultimately came to live his life in the light of his baptism. Not only did he remind himself daily of the fact of his baptism, but when he was gloomy and despondent he would shake himself back to reality by crying out, "I am baptized!"

We are people of baptism. Through water and the word we are joined for all time to the death and resurrection of Christ. Living out our baptism as faithful followers of Christ means that all we do is in response to what God has already done for, and given to, us. We constantly and continually witness to our gracious God. Our purpose in life is to go beyond ourselves in love and service. Baptism is the driving force in the life of a steward.

The baptism of Jesus may not have been understood by John, and perhaps we cannot fully understand it, but we can be certain of one thing: Jesus believed that his baptism was important, and through it took his place among those seeking to do God's will. In our baptism (and affirmation of it) we take our place among those who will live lives in response to God's gifts of self, time, and possessions—all signs of God's gracious love.

Through our baptism we begin a new history. We are reborn by water and the Spirit. We are joined forever with God and become members of God's family, the church. To use the words of the writer to the Ephesians, we "are no longer strangers and aliens, but . . . citizens with the saints and also members of the household of God" (EPHESIANS 2:19).

The *Lutheran Book of Worship* reminds us in the baptismal liturgy: "We are born children of a fallen humanity; in the waters of Baptism we are reborn children of God and inheritors of eternal life. By water and the Holy Spirit we are made members of the Church which is the body of Christ. As we live with him and with his people, we grow in faith, love, and obedience to the will of God" (*LBW*, p. 121).

Our Baptism informs our life. From it our life flows and grows. And what we receive in Baptism is a free gift, unmerited and unearned.

The writer to the Ephesians may have expressed it best when he wrote: "You were dead through trespasses and sins in which you once lived . . . But God, who is rich in mercy, out of the great love with which he loved us even when we were dead through our trespasses, made us alive together with Christ . . . For by grace you have been saved through faith, and this is not your own doing; it is the gift of God—not the result of works, so that no one may boast. For we are what he has made us, created in Christ Jesus for good works, which God prepared beforehand to be our way of life" (EPHESIANS 2:1-2a, 4-5, 8-10).

Please note those final words: *to be our way of life.* We are not saved *by*, but *for* good works. We cannot earn God's love. There is nothing we can do to merit forgiveness. God's grace is not something we can beg, borrow, buy, or steal. We do not do good works to put God in our debt. Rather, good works become our response to God's grace in our lives. And the writer to the Ephesians says that not only are these good works "to be our way of life," but that this understanding of life was "prepared beforehand" by God. In other words, good works are part of God's will for us and the way in which we live out the life God has given us.

Blessed to be a blessing

In one of the stories about Abraham and his son, Isaac, an angel of the Lord told Abraham: "By myself I have sworn, says the Lord: Because you have done this, and have not withheld your son, your only son, I will indeed bless you, and I will make your offspring as numerous as the stars of heaven and as the sand that is on the seashore. And your offspring shall possess the gate of their enemies, and by your offspring shall all the nations of the earth gain blessing for themselves, because you have obeyed my voice" (GENESIS 22:16-18). Blessed to be a blessing! That is exactly what happens to us in baptism.

Living out our baptism

Paul, writing to the church at Rome, says: "Do you not know that all of us who have been baptized into Christ Jesus were baptized into his death? Therefore we have been buried with him by baptism into death, so that, just as Christ was raised from the dead by the glory of the Father, so we too might walk in newness of life" (ROMANS 6:3-4).

God calls us to be stewards by giving us a vision of a life lived in response to God's gifts. More than a vision, it is the drive that pushes and carries us on to works of mercy, deeds of love, and the generous giving of time and possessions.

The constant threat of temptation

But what of sin? It still exists and it is for us like the thorn in St. Paul's side. We will see, as we consider Jesus' life on earth, that he had the same experience. At the very beginning of his ministry, Jesus was tempted by Satan in the wilderness. Even though Jesus was able to withstand those three temptations,

Satan did not give up. He continued to plague Jesus, tempting and opposing him time and time again throughout his earthly ministry. Sometimes the temptation was obvious, but on other occasions it was much more subtle. Well-meaning people who thought they were doing what was right were actually doing the work of Satan. Peter, chief of disciples, is a good example. At times he was Satan's unwitting spokesman. And Judas may have thought he was pushing Jesus to take action, only to discover that he had betrayed his Lord.

Inclusivity through baptism

Though we die to sin in baptism and are raised to newness of life with Christ, our lives are still filled with potholes and pitfalls. In times of temptation our baptism reminds us that we are sons and daughters of God, freed from the power of sin. Martin Luther spoke of the "priesthood of all believers." It is baptism that makes such a priesthood possible. It is baptism that equalizes and unites us.

The church is where people of all sizes and shapes, colors and ethnic backgrounds, languages and cultures, come together as the baptized family of God. This family transcends all nations, governments, political systems, ideologies, and philosophies—even time itself.

Baptism does not erase gender, or nationality, or denomination, but it unites us in Christ to give us a unique identity. And it is to such an identity that stewards call others to receive the same blessing. It is within such community that stewards work to bring others in to be blessed so they might, themselves, become a blessing to others.

The language of Paul soars when he writes to the Christians at Ephesus: "There is one body and one Spirit, just as you were called to the one hope of your calling, one Lord, one faith, one baptism, one God and Father of all, who is above all and through all and in all" (EPHESIANS 4:4-6).

Working together with Christ

We continue to be ourselves—male, female, Black, White, Hispanic, Native American, Asian—but in Christ we are one! God calls us individually, but we work with him together. Paul, writing to the Christians at Corinth, says: "As we work together with him, we urge you also not to accept the grace of God in vain" (2 CORINTHIANS 6:1). Our calling to be stewards is nothing less than to work together with Christ. There is no higher calling. Indeed, as you contemplate the meaning and scope of this fact, it looms so large as to be overwhelming. Who can totally appreciate what it means to be a co-worker with Christ? The thought is staggering, yet God never asks us to do anything for which we are not given the strength and ability.

As, together with Christ, we seek to bring the good news to the world, we do it joyfully, working hand in hand with all who are in the body of Christ. The task is ongoing. It encompasses our very lives—wherever we are, whatever we are doing.

All of life is sacred

Tuesday morning in the office and Thursday evening at the bowling alley become times of service and witness. Friday in the classroom and Saturday raking leaves become times that are seen to be just as sacred as the Sunday morning worship hour. Through baptism we are freed to live a new life, with a new perspective. The distinction between sacred and secular is seen to be artificial. All of life is sacred. All the time we are given by God is precious. If any moment, any activity, anything is profane, it is because we have profaned it. In the Genesis story of creation we are told that each time God acted, he looked at what was done and proclaimed it "good." God's intention for our lives, our world, all creation, is that it be "good." In this same vain, Jesus said that he came that we might "have life, and have it abundantly" (JOHN 10:10b).

Peace, justice, and harmony

Our stewardship calls us to work constantly for good—for peace, justice, and harmony. As followers of Christ we strive to see that the hungry are fed and the homeless sheltered. We work to end war, violence, and bloodshed. We make every effort to eliminate drug and alcohol abuse, child abuse, and the disintegration of the family. We work for safe streets, for schools that teach positive values, and congregations that are places of love. As new creatures in Christ, we will see God's creation in a new way and work toward making it what God intended it to be.

Through the power of our baptism we live lives of hope and joy. We have no more need to worry about earning salvation or appeasing an angry God. We know that God's promise is sure. We are free through our baptism to serve in God's name in all of God's world.

Jesus summed up the entire Law in two commandments: Love God with all your heart, soul, and mind, and love your neighbor as yourself. "On these two commandments," he said, "hang all the law and the prophets" (MATTHEW 22:40). These two commandments summarize our baptismal (and therefore, stewardship) response. Our lives will be characterized by love toward God on the one hand, and by love toward neighbor on the other. These two dimensions, the vertical and horizontal, will be for Christian stewards the frame of reference within which they serve.

Jesus began his ministry by being baptized. At the end, moments before his ascension, he instructed his disciples to go into all the world, teaching and baptizing. That is our mandate today as the modern counterparts of the disciples. As faithful followers we are not only called to be part of God's family, we are also called to go out and bring others to Christ so that they, too, may know God's love, be baptized, receive and recognize the gifts of God, and respond to the call to become faithful stewards.

QUESTIONS FOR REFLECTION

1. What meaning does baptism have for you? How does it affect your understanding of being a Christian steward?

2. What are some of the ways in which you can "live out" your baptism?

3. What does it mean to be saved "for, not by" good works? What are some of the good works you could be (or are) doing?

4. How can you be a "blessing" to others?

2

HOW DO YOU
DO GOD'S WILL?

Jesus is tempted by Satan

Immediately following his baptism, Jesus goes into the wilderness (desert) for forty days and forty nights. Matthew, Mark, and Luke all attest to the fact that the Spirit led Jesus into the wilderness. *Forty days and forty nights* should not be taken literally. It is a Hebrew figure of speech that simply means "an extended period of time."

What possible reason could there be for Jesus to retreat from public view in this manner? If we see Jesus' baptism as a public witness, then going to the wilderness seems somewhat out of step with his basic intention. Matthew says he went "to be tempted by the devil" (MATTHEW 4:1).

One clue that might help to explain the action of Jesus is reported by both Luke and Matthew. During that long period in the desert, Jesus fasted (MATTHEW 4:2; LUKE 4:2). This was religious discipline. It was a time for meditation and prayer. It was a time of preparation. Jesus was getting ready to begin his ministry. The question he was wrestling with was how he might accomplish God's will. What was God calling him to do and how should he do it? This, of course, is also the basic question for us as Christian stewards: What is God calling us to be and do at this time in the place where God has put us?

"Forty days" go by. Jesus is famished (MATTHEW 4:2; LUKE 4:2). Try to put yourself in Jesus' place. If you and I were in the desert—walking, sitting, thinking, praying, listening, but not eating—there would come a time when we would think

18

of nothing but food and drink. First the pangs, then the hunger. We would have a hard time concentrating. Everything would remind us of food. We'd look at the stones on the ground and wish we could eat them. The women of the villages baked small, round loaves of bread that looked much like the stones in the wilderness. Perhaps Jesus remembered the bread his mother, Mary, had baked. He might even have imagined the smell of the bread baking in a hot oven. Such thinking might well have been an open door for Satan who suggested to Jesus that he turn stones into bread (MATTHEW 4:3; LUKE 4:3).

What is God's will?

Consider this scenario. Jesus has responded to God's call. He knows that his earthly life has a specific purpose. He knows that his greatest desire is to fulfill God's will, but how should that be accomplished? Indeed, what *is* God's will? Must it not be to reach God's people, to set them straight? To turn them around? This is the basic meaning of repentance. They are lost—not in the theological sense of *damned*—but of going astray, on the wrong road, headed in the wrong direction. How can he turn them back to God's way?

During his ministry, Jesus, referring to himself as the Son of Man, told Zacchaeus that he had come "to seek out and save the lost" (LUKE 19:10). Even during this time in the wilderness he knows that he has come for a purpose. He has come to find the lost and change their direction. But first he must get their attention. How can that be done? Again, this is a question that faces us as stewards. We may want to do God's will. We may even know what God's will for us is. But how are we going to do it?

Satan—the adversary

Suddenly Satan showed up. How typical! When we are dealing with serious issues in our lives, Satan always seems close at hand. He had an answer for Jesus: "If you are the Son of God, command these stones to become loaves of bread" (MATTHEW 4:3).

In effect, Satan was saying, "Feed the people! You know
who you are, and I know who you are, but the people need
a little proof. They are hungry. They feel the same pangs you
do at this moment, but for them it is continual, day in and
day out. Feed them and they'll follow you."

Satan had a point. He always does. That's the real problem
with temptation. There is usually an element of truth—a hook
that attracts our attention. Many times the temptation seems
reasonable.

Jesus' first reaction may have been: "Well, why not? What
harm can it do? After all, they are hungry and I now know
what hunger is after being here in the wilderness for all this
time. Besides, if I feed the people they will follow me. If I
meet their physical needs—and I have the power to do it—
they will look to me, not the Romans, not the government.
Even if they don't respond to my message, at least they'll be
comfortably fed."

Temptation is serious business

So often we read or hear the story of the temptations of Jesus
and fail to consider that he may have thought seriously about
Satan's suggestions. We simply conclude that he fended off the
temptations without giving them any thought. But doesn't it
make more sense that Jesus would carefully review all his options?

Satan said, "Feed the people!" What would happen if a leader
met the physical needs of the populace? Would they not give
him their allegiance? Would they follow someone else who
might deny them pleasure and comfort? The suggestion to
turn stones into bread had merit. The people would pay attention. Then Jesus would be in a position to speak to them
and they would listen.

We need to recognize that the temptations we face in our
own lives are often well within our grasp. God gives us certain
gifts, and the temptation is to use them only for ourselves.
Selfishness may be the all-time, basic temptation with which
Satan constantly assails us. We have the choice to be selfish or
generous. But are we really making the decision on our own?

Could it not be that Satan is nearby, telling us there is nothing wrong with being selfish? "Charity begins at home," goes the old saying, and we use it to mean that we can put ourselves first. But that is a serious misinterpretation of the phrase. True charity is not to provide for our own wants to the exclusion of others, but rather that we learn the true meaning of charity at home. Charity is not directed to self; it is always used for others.

Not an earthly king

Satan's suggestion might have been of value had Jesus come to be an earthly ruler. Indeed, many earthly rulers have tried to stay in power by manipulating and satisfying the physical needs of the populace, but Jesus did not come to be that kind of king. So, he rejects the idea. After all, what would it really accomplish? He was not called to meet physical needs. He came to seek and save the lost. He was the good shepherd, sent to seek God's people and to bring them back as a shepherd brings back lost sheep.

Palestinian shepherds were excellent trackers. They could follow a trail where others saw nothing. Often they expended much effort and energy in finding a single, lost sheep. Jesus sought to do the same when it came to God's lost people. He would find each one and bring that person back. He would spare no amount of effort or energy in reaching out to sinners. God loved them all and Jesus wanted them to know it, but turning stones into bread wasn't the right way. Though it might relieve physical symptoms and prompt people to pledge earthly allegiance, it would not solve the basic problem of spiritual hunger.

"No," says Jesus to Satan. "It is written, 'One does not live by bread alone, but by every word that comes from the mouth of God'" (MATTHEW 4:4).

Satan is not a quitter

Satan, never discouraged and not to be outdone, has a second suggestion. Matthew tells us that he takes Jesus to the holy city and places him on the highest point of the Temple. "If you are the Son of God, throw yourself down," says Satan (MATTHEW 4:6).

This is the second time Satan has said, "If you are the Son of God . . ." Could it be that Jesus felt doubt? Was that voice at his baptism heard by everyone? Or was it heard only by Jesus? Did he imagine it? Perhaps Jesus began to think that he should have stayed in Nazareth, sawing and planing wood in Joseph's carpenter shop, where everything was safe, predictable, and secure.

Jesus hesitated. Any rational person would! Indeed, many persons know the fear of height. They would not even want to think about having to look down from such a place.

"What are you afraid of?" Satan taunted. "Don't you remember what is written?" Satan turned the tables on Jesus. Satan's first temptation was countered by Jesus with a quotation from Deuteronomy (8:3). Now Satan tried to beat Jesus to the punch by quoting Psalm 91:11-12. Certainly Jesus remembered it. He knew he could call upon twelve legions of angels if need be. They would swoop down and catch him before any harm came to him.

But what would he accomplish? No one else could perform such a daring feat. But would that provide sufficient reason for Jesus to do what Satan suggested? Would the people follow him because he could perform spectacular stunts? For a time perhaps, but then the awe would diminish. The crowds would want more and more spectacular feats, more and more daring demonstrations of superhuman power.

Again, Jesus said no to Satan. "It is written, 'Do not put the Lord your God to the test'" (MATTHEW 4:7).

Does this mean we should always be cautious—never take a risk? Of course not. The key is why the risk is taken. If its purpose is to enhance one's personal image and prestige—that's really what Satan was saying would happen—it should be rejected. On the other hand, if it is based on faith that God will provide, then the risk is valid.

Satan pulls out all the stops

By now we can sense Satan's frustration. His schemes weren't working. Jesus wasn't falling for them. Satan had better come up with the big one this time.

He took Jesus to a high mountain and showed him all the kingdoms of the world. "Let's make a deal," Satan said. "You can look as good as you wish in your Father's eyes; you can have any image you choose in the eyes of the world. Worship me, and with our combined power we can take over everything."

Again, we need to believe that Jesus seriously considered this offer. There is truth in Satan's words. That's why he is so dangerous. Satan's arguments are often persuasive precisely because they have an element of truth. The power of Jesus and the power of Satan together would be awesome. And it is a possibility. If it weren't, it would be no temptation. Together Satan and Jesus could take over the world, but for a third time Jesus says *no*.

"Away with you, Satan! for it is written, 'Worship the Lord your God, and serve him only'" (MATTHEW 4:10).

The mission: serve

It is in the word *serve* that Jesus finds the answer to how he will do God's will, how he will accomplish his mission. Later he told his disciples, "The Son of Man came not to be served but to serve, and to give his life a ransom for many" (MATTHEW 20:28).

Our Lord did not come to meet physical needs, perform spectacular, entertaining feats, or make powerful political deals. All of these might have brought temporary praise and adulation, but would not have been the doing of God's will.

In addition to recognizing that Jesus listened seriously to Satan's offers, we must also understand that God allowed Jesus the freedom to consider the temptations. We have the same freedom. We are not puppets whose strings are pulled by God. We have been created in a way that allows us to choose evil rather than good. It is because of God's love that we have been so created. With that same love God calls us to be stewards—to reject sin and do God's will in all things.

The role: servant

Jesus takes on the role of servant. His mission is to glorify God, not garner praise for himself from the admiring masses. Indeed, Jesus sees his mission in extreme terms. He will serve even though he may have to give his life for the *many*, a term used by Jesus to indicate the masses, that is, all the people.

Remembering the words of Isaiah, Jesus takes upon himself the role of suffering servant. In Isaiah, he finds a description of the task originally assigned to Israel. Now he will take the role upon himself. It may mean death. It will certainly mean suffering and rejection. Jesus says no to Satan and yes to God.

It ain't over 'til it's over

Is this the end of story? Is this the end of Satan and his temptations? Not at all. Luke tells us something that Matthew omits. "When the devil had finished every test, he departed from him (Jesus) *until an opportune time"* (LUKE 4:13, emphasis added).

No, it is not the end of the story. Throughout his life and ministry, temptations continue to confront Jesus. They occur when least expected and come from sources least suspected. And isn't that what you and I also experience? Satan is closest when we are most religious. Temptations come from unexpected sources and at times when we might think Satan is not even near us.

But we continue to live lives of faith, serving those in need, even if it means taking risks. Faithful stewards are dedicated and committed because they know that at the heart of things, they have been called by God and are protected by God.

John 3:16 proclaims, "God so loved the world that he gave his only Son, so that everyone who believes in him may not perish but may have eternal life." We should note at least two things in connection with this passage. First, through the action of God we are safe and, second, God shows us what we should do. "God so loved the world that he gave . . ." That is the primary characteristic of the good steward. John, in his first letter, writes, "We love because [God] first loved us" (1 JOHN 4:19). For the purposes of stewardship, we can paraphrase that to read: "We give because God first gave."

Who, me? Pledge?

Often people avoid making a financial pledge because they have no idea what the future holds. Such a position betrays a lack of faith and an unwillingness to risk believing that God will provide. Furthermore, the pledge system is nothing more than a statement of intent, allowing one to adjust a pledge as circumstances change—either up or down. When viewed from that perspective, pledging is hardly a risk.

Jesus taught that giving should have no limit. Giving time, skills, and money can only be done in the context of the giver's need to give. That is why Jesus told those listening to what we call the "Sermon on the Mount": "You have heard that it was said, 'An eye for an eye and a tooth for a tooth.' But I say to you, Do not resist an evildoer. But if anyone strikes you on the right cheek, turn the other also; and if anyone wants to sue you and take your coat, give your cloak as well; and if anyone forces you to go one mile, go also the second mile. Give to everyone who begs from you, and do not refuse anyone who wants to borrow from you" (MATTHEW 5:38-42).

The message of Jesus was always extreme, not because he was given to hyperbole, but because people seem so often to do as little as possible. Perhaps the way to shock us out of our selfishness and lethargy is to call for that which seems to be exorbitant.

As we shall see later in our story, what Jesus is willing to give on the cross is beyond calculation.

QUESTIONS FOR REFLECTION

1. What is God calling you to be and to do at this time?
2. What are some of the temptations that you are faced with? What helps you to resist them?
3. "We give because God first gave." How does this idea help you to live your life as a faithful follower of Jesus?
4. How do we determine God's will for our lives?

3

STAND BY FOR AN
IMPORTANT ANNOUNCEMENT

Jesus is ready to begin his ministry

It was Saturday, the Sabbath. Jesus was in Nazareth and he went to the synagogue. There was nothing unusual in this; it was his custom.

The synagogue was an important place. During the exile when the Jews could not worship in the Temple, they developed synagogues as places of study and worship. Even after their return from the exile and the rebuilding of the Temple, the synagogue as an institution continued.

Jesus was familiar to those in attendance. After all, he had grown up in Nazareth. People had known him since he was a small child. They had watched him grow up. He had learned carpentry in Joseph's shop. No doubt many of them had had dealings with Jesus as a carpenter. He was one of them—a "local boy," as we say.

A key moment

What makes this visit to the synagogue different is that Jesus has changed careers. He is no longer a boy—no longer a carpenter. He is now an itinerant preacher and teacher. Ever since his baptism and the subsequent clarifying of his mission, Jesus has been teaching in the synagogues of Galilee. Luke tells us that he "was praised by everyone" (LUKE 4:15).

This is his first time back home and he is honored in the synagogue by being asked to read. The leader of the synagogue would often ask visiting rabbis to read from the Scriptures. A scroll is brought to Jesus. It is the Book of Isaiah. He unrolls it, then finds and reads these words:

> The Spirit of the Lord is upon me,
> because he has anointed me to bring
> good news to the poor.
> He has sent me to proclaim release
> to the captives and recovery of
> sight to the blind,
> to let the oppressed go free,
> to proclaim the year of the
> Lord's favor (LUKE 4:18-19;
> see ISAIAH 61:1-2a).

Jesus rolls up the scroll, hands it back to the attendant, and sits down. This was the posture for preaching. All those in attendance wait to hear what he has to say. Luke put it this way: "The eyes of all in the synagogue were fixed on him" (LUKE 4:20b).

Jesus began his sermon with just nine words: "Today this scripture has been fulfilled in your hearing" (LUKE 4:21). This is his inaugural sermon, if you will. He has clearly set forth the purpose and direction of his ministry.

Initial reaction—very good!

What is the reaction of the people? They are pleased! Luke reports: "All spoke well of him and were amazed at the gracious words that came from his mouth. They said, 'Is not this Joseph's son?'" (LUKE 4:22). It seems to be part of human nature to be surprised when someone we know excels at things that we do not do as well.

When this event is reported by Matthew and Mark they add the following reactions of the audience on that day: "Where did this man get this wisdom and these deeds of power?"

(MATTHEW 13:54). "What is this wisdom that has been given to him?" (MARK 6:2).

The hometown reaction paralleled that of the rest of Galilee where Jesus had been teaching and preaching. He really was good. He spoke well. He had a good understanding of Scripture. Just think of it—the carpenter's son!

But wait . . .

Jesus was not finished. As they knew him, he knew them. He knew what they were thinking. "Doubtless," he said, "you will quote to me this proverb, 'Doctor, cure yourself!' And you will say, 'Do here also in your hometown the things that we have heard you did at Capernaum'" (LUKE 4:23).

Jesus was on the attack. It's nice that they liked his voice and wanted to praise a local person who made good, but Jesus' mission was not to seek popularity. He already rejected that idea when it was suggested by Satan in the wilderness.

Jesus didn't ask anyone to tell him how wonderful he was. "No prophet is truly accepted in his hometown," he said. "You may want to tell others you know me and gain recognition for yourselves, but that is not what my mission is about. Consider the great famine in the time of Elijah that lasted three and a half years. Was Elijah sent to the widows of Israel? Would they have listened? No! God sent him to a foreigner—the widow of Zarephath in Sidon. And what about Elisha? There were many lepers in Israel at the time, but God didn't send the prophet to them. Would they have listened? No! God sent Elisha to a Syrian—Naaman." (See LUKE 4:24-27).

On second thought . . .

The people knew these words were directed at them. They knew he was saying they were just like their forebears; that they wouldn't listen to a prophet who was right under their collective noses. And they were enraged. "They got up," says Luke, "drove [Jesus] out of the town, and led him to the brow of the hill on which their town was built, so that they might hurl him off the cliff" (LUKE 4:29). They were so angry they intended to kill him, but somehow (Luke doesn't say how) Jesus managed to get away from them and "went on his way" (LUKE 4:30).

Some reaction to a first sermon! But it shows us three things. 1) Jesus was going to tell the truth no matter what the cost. 2) He was going to stick by his decisions made in the wilderness. 3) By quoting Isaiah he indicated that his mission is primarily concerned with liberation.

Lessons for stewards

These are lessons for us as we respond to God's call to be faithful stewards in our time. We must always speak the truth and speak it boldly. Far too often the spokespersons for stewardship have been timid and overcautious. However, to be a faithful steward is not to be cowardly or hesitant. Our message should be shouted from the housetops.

Some pastors pride themselves on never preaching about money. "You never hear a stewardship sermon from my pulpit," they say. How strange. How sad. Every sermon should be a stewardship sermon if it speaks about living out our baptismal life in God's world. That is what Christian stewardship involves. Although many equate stewardship only with money, it involves much more than our financial giving. Every moment of every day is part of our stewardship response. If sermons are to be relevant they must speak to our deepest needs and relate to life as we live it. And if they do that, they must be about stewardship because at its broadest, Christian stewardship relates to all of God's gifts and thus, to all of life.

By the same token, to ignore money or to speak about it vaguely or infrequently is to miss the point of Christian stewardship. Jesus never hesitated to speak about riches. At least six of his parables deal directly with money and many of the others are closely related.

Money is one of the most common things in life. We work daily to receive it. We use money to pay our bills, buy food, and save for the future. Yet money is misunderstood. It is not an end in itself; it is merely a means to an end. Money by itself has no value. The value comes only as it is used—or misused.

Paul, writing to Timothy, says that "the love of money is a root of all kinds of evil" (1 TIMOTHY 6:10).

Money can become one's "god." The message of Jesus to "strive first for the kingdom of God and his righteousness" (MATTHEW 6:33) is in direct contrast to those who would put money first.

Jesus will not be swayed

The decision of Jesus in the wilderness was to become a servant and put that servanthood above all else, no matter what the personal cost might be. "No one has greater love than this," said Jesus to his disciples, "to lay down one's life for one's friends" (JOHN 15:13). There would be those who would try to stop Jesus from carrying out his mission. Some of them would be those closest to him. But Jesus was not to be swayed by words of advice, warnings, or even direct action. He had sorted out the possibilities, and he knew that service was the way to accomplish God's will.

Candidates for ordination in the Presbyterian Church were, at one time, asked if they would be willing to be damned for the glory of God. That is, would they be willing to give up their own salvation if in doing so they were able to glorify God. The expected answer was, yes. If they were hesitant or unwilling to answer in the affirmative, a serious question was raised in the minds of some of the examiners about their fitness to be ministers of the church.

Faithful stewards know that they may not have to sacrifice their lives in serving, but the point is one of attitude and willingness. To be willing to sacrifice one's life is what is called for, and such an attitude can be demonstrated by the generous giving of time, abilities, and resources. To listen, to help, to be available in moments of crisis is to demonstrate true Christian stewardship.

Every day we encounter people who are hurting, people who are in need of love and encouragement. To go out of our way to speak kindly, offer assistance, and genuinely care for that person is a vital part of being a steward.

Jesus never turned away anyone who came to him. His disciples at times were impatient and didn't want to be bothered. When they suggested that Jesus was too busy to see some children, he became angry. "Let the little children come to me," he said, "and do not stop them; for it is to such as these that the kingdom of heaven belongs" (MATTHEW 19:14).

A woman of remarkable faith

On one occasion, while Jesus and his little band of disciples trudged along in the district of Tyre and Sidon, a Canaanite woman caught sight of him and began to cry out: "Have mercy on me, Lord, Son of David; my daughter is tormented by a demon."

Jesus did not pay any attention to her, so she turned to the disciples and began to shout at them. This was the last thing they wanted to deal with, so they pleaded with Jesus to send her away. "I was sent only to the lost sheep of the house of Israel," Jesus told them, and continued on toward his destination. This probably made the disciples feel better. After all, the woman's ancestors were ancient enemies of the Jews. Clearly, Jesus had better things to do than deal with foreigners.

The woman, falling farther behind, shouted out: "You're not fair!" With that Jesus stopped. "What isn't fair," he said, "is to take the children's food and throw it to the dogs." "You're right, Lord," said the woman, "but even the dogs get to eat the crumbs that fall from their master's table!"

This exchange needs to be explained. The Jews often used the word *dog* in referring to the Gentiles, feeling that God probably treated dogs and Gentiles with about the same measure of concern. Jesus was certainly not demeaning the woman with this term. He was simply reflecting a common attitude to describe the situation. The woman herself did not flinch. She used the same term to say that even dogs got better treatment from their masters than Jesus seemed to be giving her. One can almost hear the laugh in Jesus' voice and sense his delight when he said to her: "Woman, great is your faith! Let it be done for you as you wish" (see MATTHEW 15:21-28).

To serve is to be free

Before Jesus fed the five thousand—as we shall see in the next chapter—the disciples were all for sending the crowds away so they could have some peace and quiet, but Jesus had other ideas. He had no intention of sending the crowds away on their own, without food. His compassionate nature simply would not allow it.

The point should be clear. Jesus had made the decision to live his life as God's servant and he would do so whether it meant inconvenience, changing plans, or doing something unexpected. Nothing deterred him. The love he came to share was too great.

During his entire ministry, Jesus would see people bound by old ideas, rigid religious observances, and laws that served only to deny them a full life. John reports that one day while teaching, "Jesus said to the Jews who had believed in him, 'If you continue in my word, you are truly my disciples; and you will know the truth, and the truth will make you free.' They answered him, 'We are descendants of Abraham and have never been slaves to anyone. What do you mean by saying, "You will be made free?"' Jesus answered them, 'Very truly, I tell you, everyone who commits sin is a slave to sin. The slave does not have a permanent place in the household; the son has a place there forever. So if the Son makes you free, you will be free indeed'" (JOHN 8:31-36). The attitude of these people is closely akin to those who had said that Jews had no need to be baptized.

Christian stewards know the freedom of the gospel and want to share that good news with all people. To those who are held in bondage by sin, to the poor, the spiritually blind, to those who are oppressed, the gospel is a message of liberation and joy. To know Christ is to know truth and freedom. The message is for all those persons in our world who are lost and confused, and who long to be truly free.

QUESTIONS FOR REFLECTION

1. How does the interpretation of the mission of Jesus in terms of liberation help us in our understanding of being stewards?

2. What are some of the ways people "love money?" How should we as Christian stewards value and use money?

3. Who are some of the people with whom we could be sharing the good news of Jesus?

4

COULD SATAN
HAVE BEEN RIGHT?

The people try to make Jesus their king

Christians often do not give Satan credit for anything except evil and deception, but we need to admit that there are times when Satan knows what he is talking about, regardless of his motives. Consider that business about feeding the people. In the wilderness, Satan had suggested that Jesus could get followers by simply turning stones into bread and feeding the people. Jesus rejected that idea, but the proof of Satan's suggestion is what happens when Jesus miraculously feeds some five thousand people.

To see the event in perspective we'll need to compare the various accounts.

It is late in the day. Matthew, Mark, and Luke all say so (MATTHEW 14:15; MARK 6:35; LUKE 9:12). John makes no mention of the time, but it is interesting to note that this is the only miracle (and one of the few incidents) reported by all four Gospel writers.

The rhythm of the steward's life

Luke tells us that Jesus and his disciples have gone to Bethsaida for some rest and relaxation (LUKE 9:10). Such times of prayer and meditation were a regular part of Jesus' life and ministry. He would take his disciples away from the hustle and bustle of daily life to recharge his (and their) spiritual and physical batteries.

This practice of Jesus suggests a rhythm of life for stewards—work, rest, work, rest. Jesus knew the value of taking a break in order to gear up for the next effort. We need to rest, study, relax, pray, think, and support one another to be fully ready to carry out the mission of Christ in the world. There is a time to take a break and a time to work. Evald B. Lawson, who for many years was president of Upsala College in East Orange, New Jersey, used to say: "The time comes when we need to get off our knees and get on our overalls." He was talking about the pattern of work, rest, work, rest.

Others first

The crowds that followed Jesus were often able to find him and his disciples, even in the most remote places. For Jesus, the call to duty was stronger than the call to rest. He rarely, if ever, turned these seekers away, no matter how tired and hungry he might be.

It was not unusual for people to tag along. Most rabbis had a close following of learners (disciples), and anyone who wished was permitted to travel along and listen to the teaching. It appears that Jesus often had a larger than usual following. John tells us that in this instance the crowd numbered five thousand (JOHN 6:10). Mark points out that there were five thousand *men* (MARK 6:44). Matthew puts it this way: "Those who ate were about five thousand men, besides women and children" (MATTHEW 14:21). John says that the "crowd kept following [Jesus] because they saw the signs that he was doing for the sick" (JOHN 6:2).

The disciples were all for getting rid of them. "Send the crowds away so that they may go into the villages and buy food for themselves," the disciples tell Jesus, but he has other ideas. "They need not go away; you give them something to eat," he says (MATTHEW 14:15-16; see also MARK 6:35-37; LUKE 9:12-13). John tells us in his version of the story that Jesus, when he saw a large crowd coming, asked Philip: "Where are we to buy bread for these people to eat?" (JOHN 6:5b). (John's explanation is that Jesus did this to test Philip.) Philip's reply helps us to see just how large the crowd really was and how much food it would take to feed them. He tells Jesus: "Six months' wages would not buy enough bread for each of them to get a little" (JOHN 6:7).

An impossible situation—or is it?

At this point the four Gospel writers agree that the only food available was two small fish and five loaves of barley bread. John supplies the information that this food came from a young lad. Barley bread was the bread of the poor. It was the cheapest of bread and scorned by the rich. The fish were no larger than sardines—probably pickled (remember they had no refrigeration so preservation of food was a real problem). Andrew asked: "What good will they be when we have so many people to feed?" (see JOHN 6:9b).

"Make the people sit down," says Jesus (JOHN 6:10; also MATTHEW 14:19, MARK 6:39, LUKE 9:14). Then he took the five loaves and two fish, looked to heaven (the people would recognize in this gesture where the power was coming from), blessed and broke them, and gave them to the disciples to distribute. When everyone had eaten (and all four writers agree that everyone ate all they wanted and perhaps more) they gathered the leftovers, which filled twelve baskets (MATTHEW 14:19-21; MARK 6:41-44; LUKE 9:16-17; JOHN 6:11-13).

What does it all mean?

How does one explain this miracle? Perhaps Jesus simply multiplied bread and fish to the extent that people could eat to excess. If that is its only meaning, then what application can it have for us today, other than being an interesting and intriguing story?

One possibility is suggested by William Barclay in his Daily Study Bible Series

> It is scarcely to be thought that the crowd left on a
> nine-mile expedition without making any preparations
> at all. If there were pilgrims with them, they would
> certainly possess supplies for the way. But it may be

that none would produce what he had, for he selfishly—and very humanly—wished to keep it all for himself. It may then be that Jesus, with that rare smile of his, produced the little store that he and his disciples had; with sunny faith he thanked God for it and shared it out. Moved by his example, everyone who had anything did the same; and in the end there was enough, and more than enough, for all.

It may be that this is a miracle in which the presence of Jesus turned a crowd of selfish men and women into a fellowship of sharers. It may be that this story represents the biggest miracle of all—one which changed not loaves and fishes, but men and women.

William Barclay, The Gospel of John (Philadelphia: Westminster, 1975) 1:204.

Whether we wish to accept Barclay's explanation or not, it points up what would, indeed, be a miracle in our time: people willing to share to the extent that world hunger could be completely eliminated. No matter how we interpret or understand this miracle of Jesus, faithful stewards will strive with all the energy and resources available to erase the problem of hunger so that no child or adult in all the world goes to bed at night with the gnawing pangs of hunger.

Satan predicted this

The people's reaction to this experience can only be guessed at if you rely on Matthew, Mark, and Luke's accounts. John, however, spells it out. "When the people saw the sign that [Jesus] had done, they began to say, 'This is indeed the prophet who is to come into the world'" (JOHN 6:14).

Is this the end of the story? Not at all. We need to continue reading, especially John's version, to see what happens. John tells us that the people want Jesus to be their king, even if they have to force him to do so. He has fed them; let him be their leader. Who else can provide for their needs like this?

John makes no mention of the temptations in his gospel account, but the very thing Satan suggested to Jesus has been proven by feeding the five thousand. "Feed the people and they will follow you" was the temptation. In the wilderness Jesus had rejected the idea as not appropriate to the way he should fulfill his mission. Now Satan's suggestion is no longer in the realm of theory or debate. The temptation has become a reality and Jesus is forced to escape the clutches of his admirers. John tells us that the retreat of Jesus into the hills was his intentional way of eluding the enthusiastic crowds who want to proclaim him king.

Jesus will do whatever it takes to be faithful

It was a master diversionary move for Jesus to send the disciples across the lake. In a crowd as large as this, many could not really see or hear what was happening. They had to rely on the movement of the crowd itself. It would have been quite logical to assume that the followers of Jesus were doing just that: *following*. John begins his account of this event by reporting that Jesus had crossed from the other side of the lake (JOHN 6:1); it would not be at all unusual for Jesus to return from whence he had come. Thus, when the disciples head back across the lake, the crowd followed (probably on foot). Jesus, in the meantime, went in the opposite direction and foiled the would-be kingmakers.

The temptation to be successful is alive in our time. Christian stewards will recognize it for what it is, but we must always be on our guard. Satan has a way of making us think that when we are doing his work, we are being faithful to God. For example, what is wrong with attracting large crowds? After all, by so doing, more will hear the good news. What is wrong with reaching out to ask people to give? The more we ask, the more will be given, and the more that is given, the more can be done.

The issue is obviously one of faithfulness, not success. The basic question for every steward is the following: "What is God calling me (or us) to be and do at this time?" Satan had some convincing arguments. There was an element of truth in what he said to Jesus, but our Lord constantly evaluated everything with God in mind, not success, not popularity, not power.

A clear and revealing contrast

"Two men went up to the temple to pray," taught Jesus, "one a Pharisee and the other a tax collector" (LUKE 18:10). His listeners—people "who trusted in themselves that they were righteous and regarded others with contempt" says Luke (18:9)—would immediately think that they knew who the "good guy" was, namely, the Pharisee. They believed tax-collectors to be the lowest scum on earth; fellow Jews who had sold out to the Romans. Not only that, they were dishonest, often bilking their brothers and sisters to line their own pockets. There would be no doubt in the minds of those listening that the Pharisee was good and the tax collector bad, or even worse.

"The Pharisee, standing by himself," says Jesus, "was praying thus, 'God, I thank you that I am not like other people: thieves, rogues, adulterers, or even like this tax collector. I fast twice a week; I give a tenth of all my income'" (LUKE 18:11-12).

Who could argue with that? He would be telling the truth. The Pharisees were the professional religionists. They tried to observe every tittle and last letter of the law. If a Pharisee said he was a tither, he was a tither. There was no need to question his veracity.

"But the tax collector," continues Jesus, "standing far off, would not even look up to heaven, but was beating his breast and saying, 'God, be merciful to me, a sinner!' I tell you, this man went down to his home justified rather than the other; for all who exalt themselves will be humbled, but all who humble themselves will be exalted" (LUKE 18:13-14).

This is a strong lesson for Christian stewards. The proof is not in our accomplishments. Tithing may be a desirable practice. We may even give much beyond ten percent. Attending church, singing hymns, saying prayers, participating in church activities, all are to be commended. But the issue is not one

of pride in ourselves, but faith in God. If tithing and involve-
ment in the work of the church is our response to the way we
have been blessed by God, then we have the proper perspective
on things. If, however, we tithe and assume positions of lead-
ership in order to be seen by others and be commended for
our good works, we have yielded to Satan's temptation.

The perfect prayer

"Whenever you pray," said Jesus in his sermon on the mount,
"do not be like the hypocrites; for they love to stand and pray
in the synagogues and at the street corners, so that they may
be seen by others. Truly I tell you, they have received their
reward. But whenever you pray, go into your room and shut
the door and pray to your Father who is in secret; and your
Father who sees in secret will reward you" (MATTHEW 6:5-6).

Luke tells us that one time while Jesus was praying "in a
certain place" the disciples came and asked him to teach them
to pray "as John [the Baptizer] taught his disciples" (LUKE
11:1). Thus, Jesus teaches them what we have come to call
the Lord's Prayer. Matthew, however, places the teaching of
this prayer in the context of the sermon on the mount. Jesus
begins by saying, "Do not heap up empty phrases as the Gentiles do; for they think that they will be heard because of their
many words. Do not be like them, for your Father knows what
you need before you ask him. Pray then in this way: Our
Father in heaven, hallowed be your name. Your kingdom come.
Your will be done, on earth as it is in heaven. Give us this day
our daily bread. And forgive us our debts, as we also have
forgiven our debtors. And do not bring us to the time of trial,
but rescue us from the evil one" (MATTHEW 6:7-13).

The Lord's Prayer is the perfect prayer for stewards. In it
we ask for all that we need to be faithful to our calling as
followers of Christ.

Our Lord certainly knew what it meant to be assaulted by
"the evil one." And he knew that with God's power and help,
temptations could be resisted. As stewards we will know times
of great temptation, but when Satan is near we can pray "deliver

us from evil" and know that the God who hears prayer answers prayer.

A song of victory!

Satan can and will keep trying, but, to quote Martin Luther's great battle hymn "A Mighty Fortress":

> Though hordes of devils fill the land
> All threat'ning to devour us,
> We tremble not, unmoved we stand;
> They cannot overpow'r us.
> Let this world's tyrant rage;
> In battle we'll engage!
> His might is doomed to fail;
> God's judgment must prevail!
> One little word subdues him.

QUESTIONS FOR REFLECTION

1. How does an understanding of Jesus' rhythm of work, rest, work, rest help us to be faithful stewards?

2. Why did the people want to make Jesus their king? Do you ever try to get God to do what you want rather than asking what it is that God wants you to do?

3. What is the difference between being successful and being faithful? How does the difference help us in our Christian stewardship?

5
WHO *IS* JESUS?

A question of major importance

W ho is Jesus?" The question is crucial to our understanding of what it means to be a Christian steward. Our answer will determine, to a great extent, how we will respond to God's good news.

Jesus had been with his disciples for almost three years. Was anybody listening? Did anyone know what he was trying to do? He needed to find out.

Matthew, Mark, and Luke all tell the story. It is not surprising that the shortest and simplest version is from Mark (8:27-30). Matthew (16:13-20) adds the account of Jesus' giving to Simon the name Peter. Luke (9:18-27) relates Jesus' conversation with the disciples about the future, what will happen, and what their reaction must be.

What are they thinking?

Prior to this story, Mark (8:14-21) and Matthew (16:5-12) tell of an incident in which the disciples have neglected to bring along enough bread. They have only one loaf. Jesus, realizing that they are puzzled, asks "Do you not yet understand?" (MARK 8:21; also see MATTHEW 16:9). It is this realization, this question of doubt, that may have prompted Jesus to find out what they were really thinking. So, while traveling through Caesarea Philippi, Jesus asks his disciples pointblank: "Who do people say that the Son of Man is?" (MATTHEW 16:13). Luke says that this question was asked "when Jesus was praying alone, with only the disciples near him" (LUKE 9:18).

Many answers

The disciples were well-positioned to answer such a question. Jesus was up front, teaching, healing, and preaching. The disciples were, no doubt, part of the audience. They could hear what was being said. Jesus asks the disciples: "Who do people say that I am?" (MARK 8:27).

One of the disciples answered immediately. "They think you are John the Baptist." Jesus considered that. It wasn't a bad answer. After all, John and Jesus were cousins. Maybe there was a family resemblance, although it is more likely that the message of Jesus sounded a great deal like John's. Indeed, Matthew tells us that when Jesus heard John had been arrested, he proclaimed, "Repent, for the kingdom of heaven has come near" (MATTHEW 4:17). That was the message of John (MATTHEW 3:2). Jesus had intentionally connected his ministry to that of John, though he did not confine it to the wilderness, wear the clothing John wore, nor eat what John ate. And, as far as we know, Jesus did not baptize. Yet, some people thought he was John.

"What else do you hear?" Jesus asked. "Many of the people are convinced you are Elijah," the disciples replied. There was some sense in this answer, too. Jesus could understand why the people might think he was Elijah. After all, they knew the word of the Lord reported by the prophet Malachi: "Lo, I will send you the prophet Elijah before the great and terrible day of the Lord comes" (MALACHI 4:5). Elijah had been taken, according to 2 Kings 2:9-12, into heaven in "a chariot of fire and horses of fire." The common, popular belief among the people was that Elijah was not dead and would return to herald the end of the world. Hearing now the message that the "kingdom is at hand" convinced many of the people that this must be Elijah.

"Is that it?" asks Jesus. "No," they reply. "Some of the people think you must be Jeremiah." Again, it is not difficult to understand why they would think so. The people believed that before the exile (586 B.C.) Jeremiah had removed the Ark and the Altar of Incense from the Temple and hidden them away for safekeeping. When the end came, Jeremiah would return, the Ark and the Altar would be restored, and there would be true worship. Much of Jesus' teaching and preaching might have led them to see him as the one who would restore the golden age of Israel.

"Anything else?" Jesus asked. "Well, there are those who really don't know who you are, but they are convinced that you must be one of the prophets come back to life." "But who do you say I am?" Jesus asked (MATTHEW 16:15). It isn't enough to know what they are saying in the back row. What about the disciples? They had more opportunities to listen to Jesus and to ask questions than anyone else. They had traveled with him, studied and worked, laughed and joked together. They had been with him in public and in private. They had prayed and struggled together. Theirs was an intimate circle of devoted friends. Who did they think he was?

Peter has the right answer!

Peter was the first to answer. "You are the Messiah," (MARK 8:29b). Matthew adds the words "the Son of the living God" (MATTHEW 16:16) and then reports Jesus' reply: "Blessed are you, Simon son of Jonah! For flesh and blood has not revealed this to you, but my Father in heaven. And I tell you, you are Peter, and on this rock I will build my church, and the gates of Hades will not prevail against it" (MATTHEW 16:17-18).

The play on words is more obvious in Greek than when translated into English. Peter is *Petros*, which means "rock." It is as if Jesus were saying, "Simon, you have correctly identified me as the son of the living God, and I you, as the son of Jonah. No human has convinced you of this. It can only come from God. And so from now on I'm changing your name to Rock. It is rocklike faith like yours that the future mission of the church will be built upon."

Who is Jesus?

To answer that Jesus was "a good man, one of the prophets," will produce one reaction; to answer with Peter that Jesus is "the Messiah, the Son of the living God" will produce another. If you claim to be a Christian because you are following the teachings of a prophet who lived some two thousand years ago and was called the Christ, your response to Jesus will be different from the person who sees Jesus as God's Son and not just an itinerant preacher who had some good ideas that we probably ought to practice in our lives.

The question demands an answer. We cannot avoid it. What we say will make all the difference. Jesus knew this, and that is why he asked the question in the first place. He would hand over his mission to his disciples in a very short time, and he wanted to be certain that they knew, as we say, "what was what." As good stewards, we need to be very clear who Jesus is, whose we are, and what our mission is all about.

A trap

Everyday events often afforded Jesus an opportunity to teach. On one occasion, shortly before the end of his earthly ministry, the Pharisees decided on a plan to trip up Jesus. Although they were not willing to act directly, they plotted to send "their disciples . . . along with the Herodians, saying, 'Teacher, we know that you are sincere, and teach the way of God in accordance with truth, and show deference to no one; for you do not regard people with partiality'" (MATTHEW 22:15-16).

These words for Jesus would have been tantamount to waving a red flag. There came Satan again with one more temptation! Satan kept finding opportune times to assail Jesus. He was, moreover, very subtle, using these religious leaders, giving them soft words about Jesus' sincerity, his teaching of God's truth, and his impartiality. We must always be on guard. Often behind words of praise can be Satan's purposes. Even worse can be the human desire to hear words of praise, gain the spotlight, and achieve popularity. Few things smack so much of selfishness than the constant quest for adulation.

Of course, Jesus saw through the whole thing. The very fact that the Pharisees and Herodians were linked showed him that something was going on.

"Tell us," they continued, "what you think. Is it lawful to pay taxes to the emperor, or not?" (MATTHEW 22:17). Then Jesus knew what they were up to. The Pharisees deeply resented paying tax to an earthly ruler because they thought it took loyalty away from God. The Herodians were the ones who had compromised with Rome in order to stay in power. They were the ones who, in a sense, allowed Rome to levy the taxes against the people. Jesus knew that his answer might be used against him. If he said, "No, it is not lawful," they could have charged with not being loyal to Rome. That could have been dangerous, for Rome did not take kindly to its enemies. On the other hand, if he said, "Yes, it is lawful," they could have charged him with disloyalty to his own people—a friend of the Romans and the hated tax collectors, and be discredited in the sight of the people. The conspirators felt that at last they had Jesus where they wanted him. Either way they would be able to get rid of him.

Jesus turns the tables

"Why are you putting me to the test, you hypocrites?" Jesus asked. "Show me the coin used for the tax." Someone produced a denarius and handed it to Jesus. He looked at it, turned it over, and held it up. "Whose head is this, and whose title?" he asked them. They answered, "The emperor's." "Then," said Jesus, "give to the emperor the things that are the emperor's, and to God the things that are God's." That wasn't what they were anticipating. The answer amazed them, says Matthew, and having no alternate plan of attack they were forced to leave Jesus and go away (see MATTHEW 22:18-22).

When Satan first assailed Jesus it was in the wilderness. By this time the temptations were coming in public, in full view of all the people. The purpose was plain. Let Jesus condemn himself by his own words and let the people be the witnesses.

In God's image

Jesus' answer stopped the Pharisees and Herodians dead in their tracks. They could not argue with what he said. They were required to pay their taxes whether they liked it or not; and, they constantly preached loyalty to God. The answer of Jesus covered both categories.

The coin with Caesar's image on it meant that it was Caesar's. One of the first things ancient kings and emperors did was to mint coinage with their image on it so as to confirm their reign. The coins were used in everyday business transactions but were, in the final analysis, always held to be the property of the ruler whose image they bore.

Using this fact, Jesus not only took the wind out of the sails of his attackers, he also taught an important lesson. If we are created in the image of God (GENESIS 1:27) then what we render to God is our very selves. We always belong to the king who "minted" us. We belong to the one whose image we bear. Paul put it this way: "I appeal to you therefore, brothers and sisters, by the mercies of God, to present your bodies as a living sacrifice, holy and acceptable to God, which is your spiritual worship. Do not be transformed by this world, but be transformed by the renewing of your minds, so that you may discern what is the will of God—what is good and acceptable and perfect" (ROMANS 12:1-2).

It has been said that money is "minted self." In other words, what we do with the time and abilities God has given us in our daily work is translated into coinage that may bear the stamp of the nation, but in reality represents our God-given inspiration, energy, and perspiration. We, who are stamped with God's image, use God's gifts to earn our paycheck. Thus, when we give money—to the church, to any charitable cause— we are giving, in reality, our selves. Indeed, no matter what we invest our money in, for good or ill, we are investing our selves. No matter how we spend our money, we are spending our selves.

To the question, "Who is Jesus?" we, as stewards, must add the knowledge and conviction of "whose we are." Created in the image of God, we must give ourselves to God and be open to God's will in ascertaining and carrying out the mission given to us.

Living with global awareness—and more

We live in a time when the world is torn by war and rumors of war. There is hunger and violence. Social ills are all around us. The problems of the environment threaten the existence of the earth itself. At one time we saw ourselves as residents of a community, state, province, or nation. More recently we have developed a global awareness. Marshall McLuhan was one of the first to present a vision of the "global village." But even that vision is too limited. We must now see ourselves as planetary pilgrims who have a place in God's universe. For centuries the church has, at the graveside of its faithful departed members, used the traditional phrase "earth to earth, ashes to ashes, dust to dust" to describe our human condition. With our current scientific understanding of the cosmos, it might be more accurate to say we come from stardust and to stardust we will return.

Stewards have a mission as close to home as the local neighborhood and as extensive as the universe itself. We, ourselves, may not go beyond our own neighborhood, but through our prayers and support for the programs of the church on community, regional, national, and international levels we are part of a wider ministry.

Few of us will venture beyond the confines of this planet, and those who do, at least for the foreseeable future, will go only a relatively short distance. Yet the breathtaking fact of this blue planet swimming in a sea of darkness, separated by light years from the nearest galaxy produces a sense of awe when we think of the Creator who loves us personally and individually.

To be a faithful steward in our time is to minister to the hungry down the street, send help to those around the world, and pray to the God of all creation with the vital sense of being on a planetary pilgrimage. In the final analysis we need to know who Jesus is, who God is, who and whose we are.

QUESTIONS FOR REFLECTION

1. Who is Jesus? Why do you want to be a faithful follower of Jesus?

2. What does it mean to have a "rocklike" faith? Does it mean that we never question or doubt anything? How does such faith help us in our Christian stewardship?

3. To be created in God's image means to belong to God. Do others see that when they look at us? If not, what should we do?

6
MORE TEMPTATIONS

Satan doesn't give up

Matthew, Mark, and Luke all report that Jesus sternly ordered his disciples to say nothing about the conversation in which he asked them who the people and they themselves thought he was. Jesus said it was too soon—that some things needed to happen before everything would be in perspective: "The Son of Man must undergo great suffering, and be rejected by the elders, chief priests, and scribes, and be killed, and on the third day be raised" (LUKE 9:22).

Luke then adds these words of Jesus: "If any want to become my followers, let them deny themselves and take up their cross daily and follow me. For those who want to save their life will lose it, and those who lose their life for my sake will save it. What does it profit them if they gain the whole world, but lose or forfeit themselves?" (LUKE 9:23-25). Jesus had figured this out in the wilderness. There he had refused to worship Satan who had promised him the world. It was not an option for Jesus to forfeit his faithfulness to God, even to gain the whole world.

Peter thinks he knows best

Peter didn't like what he heard. "Over my dead body!" he roared. If this were a motion picture, we would first see Peter's face and hear his outburst. Then we would be shown Peter from Jesus' vantage point. Peter's face would dissolve into the image of Satan. "Get behind me, Satan!" Jesus said. "For you are setting your mind not on divine things but on human things" (MARK 8:33).

This man is the same Simon who was recently so highly regarded by Jesus that his name was changed to Peter, or "Rock." But this time Jesus did not call him Simon, or Peter, or Cephas (Aramaic for "rock"), but *Satan*. Peter conjured up for Jesus the image of Satan. Jesus was transported back to the wilderness. Here was still another temptation. Here was Satan standing in his way. Here was another attempt to dissuade him from carrying out his mission of faithfulness to God's will. It was just one more example of Satan looking for "an opportune time" (LUKE 4:13b).

An ordinary man might have become discouraged and angry. Would Peter ever understand? True, he had correctly identified Jesus as the Messiah and Son of God, but in this episode Peter showed that he really didn't yet understand the mission of the Messiah.

Good intentions

There is little doubt that Peter's heart was in the right place. However, one can be sincere and still be wrong. Paul is perhaps the best example of this. Before his conversion and his name change, Saul was a zealous persecutor of the early church. He traveled extensively with legal documents that gave him the authority to arrest and bring up on charges those persons who were "followers of The Way" (as early Christianity was called). Saul was dedicated and faithful. He believed he was doing God's will, but he was wrong. It is not enough to be sincere. It was Paul's good fortune that he was stopped on his way to Damascus by the power of God, and that through this experience he was converted. The former persecutor became one of the early church's chief spokesperson, giving the rest of his life to proclaim the gospel and establish congregations.

Paul knew he was forgiven and that he had been singled out by God to be a powerful witness for Christ. But he never lost sight of humility. It was a lesson he had learned the hard way. To Timothy he wrote: "The saying is sure and worthy of full acceptance, that Christ Jesus came into the world to save sinners—of whom I am the foremost. But for that very reason I received mercy, so that in me, as the foremost, Jesus Christ might display the utmost patience, making me an example to those who would come to believe in him for eternal life" (1 TIMOTHY 1:15-16). Faithful stewards who receive and know God's mercy respond by engaging in the same mission.

Are the disciples ready?

Jesus wondered not only about Peter, but about the rest of the disciples as well. Would they ever understand? Jesus had chosen each of them carefully and by now they had been with him for almost three years. Well, given enough time they would understand, but at this moment they had little understanding of what Jesus—and they—would go through.

Would we have been as blind as the disciples? Most of us believe that we would have seen the truth. But how can we be certain? What if the earthly ministry of Jesus were taking place in the twentieth century? Who might the disciples be? Although one can only speculate, it is instructive to think about such a question.

Well-known names spring to mind, but upon reflection we must admit that the twelve disciples were not people of fame and fortune. One was a tax collector, and we can safely assume that even if he were known, it was not with generous feeling. Several were fishermen. They were probably weather-beaten, rough-and-tumble seafaring men. Poorly educated, they had to work hard with little guarantee of safety or success. Some, as far as scholars can tell, may even have been militant nationalists. That would make them angry and not always sympathetic. They were real people who worked hard to make a living. They had grown up with little or no education. They had their likes and dislikes—their strengths and weaknesses. In a nutshell, they were like you and me.

Take up your cross

Who might Jesus choose as disciples today? You? Me? Incredible as it may seem, this is the case. You and I are called by our Lord to be faithful followers. You and I serve as the modern counterparts of the original disciples of Jesus. The mission he gave to them he gives to us. To us he says, "Take up your cross and follow me daily."

What does it mean to take up one's cross? It means being willing to face and endure whatever God calls us to be and do. Persons who were executed by crucifixion were required to carry to the location of their punishment the crosses upon which they would die. It was not only a difficult physical struggle. It must have been a terrifying experience as well. With each step, the person would become more and more aware that the end of life was near. And that end would be torture. Yet there was no turning back. The cross had to be borne, the inevitable faced. Jesus told his disciples, and us, that faithfulness demands facing whatever God places before us. Christian stewards must be faithful to the end, bearing whatever joys and sorrows come our way.

The early church faced severe persecution. There were those whose will buckled under the pressure of the Roman authorities. But the ideal of faithfulness was upheld as the ultimate goal. In Revelation, the Holy Spirit tells John to write to the congregation at Smyrna, "Beware, the devil is about to throw some of you into prison so that you may be tested, and for ten days you will have affliction. Be faithful unto death, and I will give you the crown of life" (REVELATION 2:10). Being faithful unto death was not only the rallying cry. It was the standard by which dedication and commitment were judged. There was no halfway point. The early church was in a life and death struggle. To take up one's cross was a daily demand. To be faithful unto death was the standard. Without Jesus, such faithfulness was impossible. With God, however, all things were possible.

Take my yoke upon you

The demand to take up one's cross and follow Jesus is ours today. It is not an impossible demand. On our own, using our own strength, it would be impossible, but by believing and relying on Jesus, it is possible to take up one's cross and find it is not the burden that such imagery suggests. "Come to me, all you that are weary and are carrying heavy burdens," says Jesus, "and I will give you rest. Take my yoke upon you, and learn from me; for I am gentle and humble in heart, and you will find rest for your souls. For my yoke is easy, and my burden is light" (MATTHEW 11:28-30).

Jesus often used illustrations and made reference to his days as a carpenter. How well he knew, for example, the sensation of getting sawdust in one's eye. It might be only a speck, but it could feel like a log! Jesus may have known about yokes at first hand, having made them in the carpenter shop. Yokes were used to link oxen so they could work together effectively. In speaking of his yoke, Jesus was inviting us to be linked with him and to work with him. To say his yoke is easy, is another way of saying that it fits well. Being yoked with Jesus means carrying our cross, facing whatever is to come; *easy* means that the fit is perfect.

With Jesus at our side, our "yoke" (stewardship) becomes easy and natural. It is never a burden. It becomes a joy. Tithing—that is, giving ten percent of one's income for Christ's mission—is something the steward seeks to do with excitement and anticipation. If you are a tither, you know this. If you know any tithers, you have heard them tell you of its meaning for their lives. And once you tithe, it is for life. How many ex-tithers do you know?

Be on your guard

Just as Jesus and his disciples knew the tempting power of Satan, so do you and I. Satan looked for opportune times to trip up Jesus, and he continues to prey upon us.

Peter learned the lesson the hard way. In later years he gave this advice to the readers of his first letter: "Cast all your anxiety on [God], because he cares for you. Discipline yourselves, keep alert. Like a roaring lion your adversary the devil prowls around, looking for someone to devour" (1 PETER 5:7-8). These are the words of a man who knew from bitter personal experience the assaults of Satan—and the agony of having denied Jesus.

The good news is . . .

The world we live in is not sympathetic to the mission of Jesus. Many people do not want to hear the "good news." Often they have been confronted by well-meaning individuals who grabbed them by the collar to ask, "Have you been saved?" I suspect that most of the people you and I know want to steer clear of such encounters, and they don't want us to "talk religion" either. So what do we do?

In the words of an ancient eastern proverb, "a picture is worth ten thousand words." Perhaps, the life of a faithful Christian steward speaks more eloquently than all the sermons and testimonies that we can muster.

Marshall McLuhan is credited with the phrase "the medium is the message." That is, the way in which something is communicated makes more of an impression than what is being said. As a child in Sunday school, I had a teacher named Carl Carlson. He wasn't very different from other men. He had a wife and family. He worked daily to support them. On Sundays he came to teach our class. I don't remember a single lesson he taught us, but I remember Carl Carlson. He was the message. It was a message of love and concern, of sympathy and, especially, of faithfulness.

Jesus is the prime example of the medium that is the message. Jesus is at the very heart of our stewardship. He is the focal point of our understanding of our call to mission. His life is not merely an example, it *is* the good news.

They must understand!

A nagging concern for Jesus was the degree to which the disciples knew and understood that which was in store for him and for them. As his earthly ministry drew to a close, he seized opportunities to test and teach them. One day he said: "Do not let your hearts be troubled. Believe in God, believe also in me. In my Father's house there are many dwelling places. If it were not so, would I have told you that I go to prepare a place for you? And if I go and prepare a place for you, I will come again and will take you unto myself, so that where I am, there you may be also. And you know the way to the place where I am going" (JOHN 14:1-4).

Did Jesus really believe that they knew? Or, was he merely hoping that by this time something had sunk in? Was he stating a fact or simply testing their faith and understanding? Whatever his intention, Thomas speaks for all the disciples when he says, with some frustration: "Lord, we do not know where you are going. How can we know the way?" (JOHN 14:5). Is that true, or did Thomas simply want more information to confirm what he hoped was true?

Jesus spoke plainly to Thomas and the other disciples: "I am the way, and the truth, and the life. No one comes to the Father except through me. If you know me, you will know my Father also. From now on you do know him and have seen him" (JOHN 14:6-7). The medium truly is the message.

The good news that you and I have as stewards is Jesus Christ himself. He is our example, our inspiration, our savior, our Lord. We live our lives in response to him. His mission is our mission, given to us to carry out through the power of the Holy Spirit.

QUESTIONS FOR REFLECTION

1. Do you ever realize that you may not be doing what God wants you to do? What do you do then?

2. What does it mean to take up one's cross? How do you go about doing that?

3. Does the idea of putting on the yoke of Jesus have meaning for you? How? And what, then, will you do?

4. If the mission of Jesus is now our mission, what shall we do to accomplish it?

7

A ROYAL WELCOME

Moses and Elijah greet Jesus

It had been a week or so since Jesus had asked his disciples who they thought he was (see LUKE 9:28). It was one of those times when Jesus needed to be alone. It wasn't unusual. He regularly took time in order to pray, meditate, and regain his strength and resolve. Jesus took Peter, James, and John with him. This also was not unusual. These three seemed to form an inner circle that participated in events which did not include the other disciples.

The four go to a nearby mountain where no one will disturb them. "While [Jesus] was praying," reports Luke, "the appearance of his face changed, and his clothes became dazzling white" (LUKE 9:29). Mark notes: "such as no one on earth could bleach them" (MARK 9:3). This is Mark's way of saying that what is happening is of God. Matthew tells it most dramatically: "And he was transfigured before them, and his face shone like the sun, and his clothes became dazzling white" (MATTHEW 17:2).

Suddenly the disciples were startled to realize that they were not alone. Moses and Elijah were talking with Jesus! Of the three Gospel writers who report this incident, only Luke attempts to explain what Moses and Elijah were doing there: "They appeared in glory and were speaking of his departure, which he was to accomplish at Jerusalem" (LUKE 9:31). Could it be that Luke was essentially correct, except that Jesus' departure, as he puts it, was to occur here and now rather than

later? Luke was writing some 40 or 50 years after the event
and he already knew what had happened. But at this particular
moment might not Moses and Elijah be serving as a welcoming
committee from heaven? Was this the time for Jesus' royal
welcome back to heaven? Let's take a look.

The law and the prophets

Moses and Elijah are essential clues to what is happening.
Moses represents the law. The people believed he had received
what we call the Ten Commandments directly from God on
Mount Sinai (see EXODUS 34:27-28). Indeed, he had had the
experience of being transfigured while in the presence of God
(see EXODUS 34:29-35). Elijah, on the other hand, represents
the prophets. It was Elijah who was expected to return "before
the great and terrible day of the Lord" (MALACHI 4:5b).

Together, Moses and Elijah represent the law and the prophets. In the sermon on the mount, Jesus said to his listeners:
"Do not think that I have come to abolish the law or the
prophets; I have come not to abolish but to fulfill" (MATTHEW
5:17). That phrase, "the law and the prophets," referred to the
totality of Jewish religion. What is it that Jesus came to fulfill?
Perhaps it is best explained by what God told Moses: "Now
therefore, if you obey my voice and keep my covenant, you
shall be my treasured possession out of all the peoples. Indeed,
the whole earth is mine, but you shall be for me a priestly
kingdom and a holy nation" (EXODUS 19:5-6a).

The perennial problem for the people of Israel was that they
continually broke their covenant with God. However, although
they were not always faithful, they celebrated their conviction
that they were God's chosen people.

Isaiah's vision of Israel was that of God's suffering servant.
This did not mean that Israel had to suffer; it meant that Israel,
to be faithful, needed to be *willing* to suffer if that was the
cost of serving (see ISAIAH 42:1—53:12).

For our scenario, then, Jesus comes and chooses the way of
the servant, willing to suffer if need be. In a real sense, Jesus
himself took on the role that had originally been assigned to
Israel, and he succeeded. Whereas Israel had so often been

unfaithful, breaking covenant after covenant, Jesus proved to be steadfast. He fulfilled the law and the prophets. That is, he lived up to that which Israel was supposed to live up to. And now Moses and Elijah came to welcome him to heaven. Jesus is the only person who has ever fully lived a life the way God wanted it to be lived. There is no record of anything like this because it had never happened before.

Peter has an idea!

In the holiness of this momentous occasion, Peter made a suggestion. "Lord," he said, "how good it is for us to be here. We need to commemorate this event. I have an idea. We'll build three monuments right here on this very spot so people for all time will know that you and Moses and Elijah met here" (see MATTHEW 17:4). While Peter is still formulating his idea, a bright cloud overshadows the scene and Peter's speech is cut off by a thunderous voice out of the cloud: "This is my Son, the Beloved; with him I am well pleased; listen to him!" (MATTHEW 17:5). It is the same voice and the same message that was heard at the time of Jesus' baptism. Three words are added: "Listen to him!" God seems to be saying to Peter, "Be quiet! We don't need to hear from you at this time. My Son, the Beloved, is making a decision. We need to listen to him; not you, Peter."

The disciples are frightened. They fall to the ground "overcome by fear" (MATTHEW 17:6). Everything became quiet. "Suddenly," says Mark, "when they looked around, they saw no one with them any more, but only Jesus" (MARK 9:8).

It is interesting to note that although the voice from the cloud seemed to suggest that Jesus was about to speak, no words are reported. Yet all who are there know that something momentous has taken place.

Peter remembers

In later years, Peter will refer to the event when he writes: "For we did not follow cleverly devised myths when we made known to you the power and coming of our Lord Jesus Christ, but we had been eyewitnesses of his majesty. For he received honor and glory from God the Father when that voice was conveyed to him by the Majestic Glory, saying, 'This is my Son, my Beloved, with whom I am well pleased.' We ourselves heard this voice come from heaven, while we were with him on the holy mountain" (2 PETER 1:16-18). Note that Peter conveniently forgets the part where the voice from the cloud tells him to be quiet.

Yet, in a sense, if Peter had not spoken up, perhaps the outcome would have been different. As Jesus talked with Moses and Elijah, it was Peter who interrupted. It is as if time had interrupted eternity; the human had invaded the divine! Even God can't ignore it. The voice tells Peter not to speak.

If Jesus leaves, then what?

Jesus sees and hears what is going on. What will happen to these three? And the other nine? And the rest of humanity if Jesus accepts this honor and glory?

The answer is that you and I would merely have an example, not a Savior. The message of the church would not be justification by grace through faith, but something like: "Remember Jesus. He lived a sinless life. Now you go and do the same. He showed you it could be done. Now it's up to you to follow in his footsteps." If that were the message, you and I would be doomed to constant failure. We wouldn't fare any better than the Jews did in being faithful to the various covenants God made with them.

If Jesus had accepted the honor at that time, there would have been no cross, no resurrection, no new covenant—a covenant which you and I cannot break because God sealed it for all time with the blood of Jesus.

Jesus turned his back on the royal welcome and headed for Jerusalem. He knew what lay ahead, but there was no turning back. He was determined, and his disciples went with him. They were fearful and reluctant, but nevertheless they went with him.

Christian stewards follow where Christ leads

There are times when we may be reluctant. There may be times when we will be fearful. But all that will dissipate if we remember that we are not alone. Indeed, we are called to follow our Lord. Jesus did not send the disciples to Jerusalem on their own. He led them. They went with him.

We are not asked to take up our cross and try to work things out on our own. We are called to take up our cross daily and to follow our Lord where he leads.

Jesus often leads us to places we ourselves might never have thought of. Often we are asked to do things which we ourselves might have been reluctant to do. Yet relying on God's wisdom and God's will, faithful followers of Jesus find the strength, courage, and ability to do more than they might have imagined.

Show us the Father

When Jesus told his disciples that he was the way, the truth, and the life, he observed that they had already seen the Father. Philip wasn't convinced, or perhaps he just didn't understand what Jesus was saying. "Lord," he says, "show us the Father, and we will be satisfied" (JOHN 14:8). Here is that same problem again. Will they ever understand? Could it be that somehow Satan is at work tempting the disciples not to believe or understand?

"Have I been with you all this time, Philip, and you still do not know me?" asks Jesus. And putting it so plainly that no one can misunderstand, he says: "Whoever has seen me has seen the Father." Jesus then says, "How can you say, 'Show us the Father'? Do you not believe that I am in the Father and the Father is in me? The words that I say to you I do not speak on my own; but the Father who dwells in me does his works. Believe me that I am in the Father and the Father is in me; but if you do not, then believe me because of the works themselves. Very truly, I tell you, the one who believes in me will also do the works that I do and, in fact, will do greater works than these, because I am going to the Father. I will do whatever you ask in my name, so that the Father may be glorified in the Son. If in my name you ask me for anything, I will do it" (JOHN 14:9-14).

The basis for our stewardship

We are called to do the works of Jesus—even greater works, he says—but it will not be with our strength, but his. All we need to do is to ask in his name and he will do it. The phrase "in Jesus' name" is commonly used, but not well understood by many people. It means "in the way Jesus would do it." That is, when we pray in Jesus' name, we are praying the way Jesus would pray. It has been suggested that instead of ending our prayers with this phrase, we ought to begin them with it. Then many of the foolish petitions we pray would die unuttered.

Faithful stewards see their mission in terms of being faithful followers of Jesus. That is, we see our faith as incomplete if it is not lived out in words and deeds of service. Some people have had trouble with the letter of James. At the time of the Reformation, the Roman Catholic church used it heavily in promoting good works. Martin Luther called James "an epistle of straw," not because he had no regard for it as Scripture, but because of its misuse by the church. Yet James might well be described in our time as the "letter to stewards." Its message that "faith apart from works is barren" and faith "brought to completion by the works" (JAMES 2:20,22) is a message that is not only helpful, but accurate in describing the attitude and stance of Christian stewards.

"What good is it, my brothers and sisters," asks James, "if you say you have faith but do not have works? Can faith save you?" (JAMES 2:14). If we should quote James 2:14 out of context and fail to see where he is leading us, we miss his real point. "If a brother or sister is naked and lacks daily food, and one of you says to them, 'Go in peace; keep warm and eat your fill,' and yet you do not supply their bodily needs, what is the good of that? So faith by itself, if it has no works, is dead" (JAMES 2:15-17).

When we are called by God to be faithful followers of Jesus, once we know the love and mercy of God, we cannot but overflow with such blessings that we become a blessing to others. If we claim faith and yet have no regard for the plight of our neighbors, the environment, the world, the universe, we are not telling the truth. To reach out, to help, is the result of being loved. "We love," says John, "because [God] first loved us. Those who say, 'I love God,' and hate their brothers or sisters, are liars; for those who do not love a brother or sister whom they have seen, cannot love God whom they have not seen. The commandment we have from [God] is this: those who love God must love their brothers and sisters also" (1 JOHN 4:19-21). This is really what James was saying, but with different words. Paul is also saying essentially the same thing in 1 Corinthians: "If I speak in the tongues of mortals and of angels, but do not have love, I am a noisy gong or a clanging cymbal" (13:1).

As Jesus deliberately took on the role of suffering servant to be faithful to his mission, so we as good stewards are called to the same kind of willing service. Perhaps it is a cliche, but the old saying, "Practice what you preach," is essential for stewards. It is never enough merely to say the right words. We must also be willing to put our words into action.

QUESTIONS FOR REFLECTION

1. Where do you think God is leading you in your life at this time?

2. Jesus told his disciples (and therefore us) that they would do even greater works than he did. What does this mean for you? What are some of the good works you do now or could be doing?

3. Do you practice what you preach? If "actions speak louder than words," what is your witness to others?

8

ANOTHER ROYAL WELCOME

Jesus rides into Jerusalem

It is obvious that Jesus prearranged his entrance into Jerusalem. It was what we might call an action parable; not words in the usual sense of telling a story, but a message acted out.

Arrangements had been worked out to get a donkey with a simple exchange of agreed-upon phrases to ensure that the right people were getting the right donkey. "Go into the village ahead of you," Jesus said to two of his disciples, "and immediately as you enter it, you will find tied there a colt that has never been ridden; untie it and bring it. If anyone says to you, 'Why are you doing this?' [the first phrase] just say this, [the proper answer] 'The Lord needs it and will send it back here immediately'" (MARK 11:2-3).

The disciples did as Jesus directed them. It happened just as he had said, and they brought the donkey back with them. He mounted the animal and rode into Jerusalem. Many people who were spectators began to "spread their cloaks on the road and others spread leafy branches that they had cut in the fields. Then those who went ahead and those who followed were shouting, 'Hosanna! Blessed is the one who comes in the name of the Lord! Blessed is the coming kingdom of our ancestor David! Hosanna in highest heaven!'" (MARK 11:8b-10).

Jesus came in peace

Jesus knew what the people were thinking and what they wanted, but he also knew what he was doing. The two, of course, were not the same. By coming on a donkey, he came in peace. It was a sign the people recognized. They had seen kings come on donkeys and horses. The donkey was a symbol of peace; the horse a symbol of war. Jesus did not come to start a revolution, make war, or overthrow the government. He came in peace, but he came as a king. It was a parable acted out. He did not need to say a single word. The spectators saw the message.

What the people saw

The people welcomed and acclaimed Jesus as an earthly ruler. Matthew reports that when Jesus "entered Jerusalem, the whole city was in turmoil, asking 'Who is this?' The crowds were saying, 'This is the prophet Jesus from Nazareth in Galilee'" (MATTHEW 21:10-11). As they saw it, the golden age of Israel was about to be restored. Their shouts were shouts of acclaim for a king who would throw off the Roman yoke of oppression. Indeed, it is not farfetched to suggest that the crowds were being stirred up by militant nationalists (zealots) who had been convinced by Judas Iscariot that Jesus was the man to lead a revolution.

Most worldly kings wield great power and symbolize that power with fearsome weapons. In the twentieth century nations have used naval power, air power, tanks, and nuclear bombs as symbols of their immense capacity for making war, and as such, symbols of power. The intent is always to point out their superiority. They are in charge because they have the weapons to beat others into submission. Jesus carried no sword and discouraged those who did. His kingdom—God's kingdom—was and is based on love, not violence. The only throne Jesus would occupy would be found in human hearts.

Luke reports that there were some Pharisees who wanted to put a stop to the whole thing. Whether they were opposed to the zealots or sympathetic to Jesus is difficult to say, but they said to him, "Teacher, order your disciples to stop." But Jesus knew that could not be. "I tell you," he said, "if these [people] were silent, the stones would shout out" (LUKE 19: 39-40).

John quotes some of the Pharisees talking among them-selves: "You see, you can do nothing. Look, the world has gone after him!" (JOHN 12:19). John also tells us that "many, even of the authorities, believed in him. But because of the Pharisees they did not confess it, for fear that they would be put out of the synagogue; for they loved human glory more than the glory that comes from God" (JOHN 12:42-43).

Clearly, one of Satan's favorite ploys is to appeal to the human desire for praise and approval. The first two temptations in the wilderness were aimed at popularity. "Feed the people, do spectacular stunts, and the people will love you," says Satan. These temptations were not reserved for Jesus. The Pharisees were thus tempted and such temptations come our way as well. Faithful followers of Jesus will recognize the temptation and seek to avoid popularity and success as ends in themselves. The only one who needs to see and approve of what we do is God. If we are faithful in doing God's will, we will have achieved far more than society's approval.

The people knew the oracle of the prophet Zechariah:

> Rejoice greatly, O daughter Zion!
> Shout aloud, O daughter Jerusalem!
> Lo, your king comes to you;
>   triumphant and victorious is he.
> humble and riding on a donkey,
>   on a colt, the foal of a donkey.
> He will cut off the chariot from Ephraim
>   and the war horse from Jerusalem;
> and the battle bow shall be cut off,
>   and he shall command peace to the nations;
> his dominion shall be from sea to sea,
>   and from the River to the ends
>   of the earth (ZECHARIAH 9:9-10).

Many would have remembered the references to war, while Jesus, no doubt with this prophecy fixed in his mind, rode into Jerusalem wanting to emphasize peace.

The next day

Jesus and his disciples went to the Temple. What he found there angered him. He began to overturn the tables of the moneychangers. In the eyes of the zealots this must have been a puzzling action. Had the revolt started? If so, this was a strange way to begin. The revolution was not aimed at the people or their religious practices; it was targeted at the Romans. Of what possible value was this action against the moneychangers?

"Is it not written," asked Jesus, quoting ISAIAH 56:7, " 'My house shall be called a house of prayer for all the nations'? But you have made it a den of robbers" (MARK 11:17).

This kind of talk made the zealots uneasy. Had Judas misled them? It certainly did not sound like the talk of one who would get rid of the Romans. Yet the general public was fascinated. Mark reports that "when the chief priests and the scribes heard [what Jesus had said], they kept looking for a way to kill him; for they were afraid of him, because the whole crowd was spellbound by his teaching" (MARK 11:18).

The kingdom is not a place

Jesus spent most of his ministry speaking about the kingdom of God. Perhaps this emphasis misled the people into thinking that he was talking about some kind of earthly kingdom. In reality, he was talking about the ancient Jewish idea that in the final analysis Israel had only one king: God. No title for God in the Old Testament is used more frequently than king. The Book of Psalms is replete with references to God as king. The only reason Israel ever had a human king was that the people looked at neighboring nations and demanded to have what they had. Their wish was granted and Saul became the first king (see 1 SAMUEL 8-9). The prophet Samuel, however, rebuked them, telling them that by demanding a king they had rejected God. Israel was a theocracy; that is, God was their ruler in both the religious and political realms.

When Jesus spoke of the kingdom of God, he was speaking of God's ultimate rule in the lives of the people. He was reminding them of their ancient religious roots. He was calling them to the very foundations of their faith. Another phrase used by Jesus, interchangeable with "kingdom of God" was "kingdom of heaven." This phrase may be less susceptible to misinterpretation because it cannot be interpreted in worldly political terms.

As we said earlier, Matthew reports that Jesus began his ministry with the very words used by his cousin, John: "Repent, for the kingdom of heaven has come near" (MATTHEW 3:2, 4:17). Mark reports it this way: "The time is fulfilled, and the kingdom of God has come near; repent, and believe in the good news" (MARK 1:15). Repentance implies change; a turning around, going in the right direction. We surrender ourselves to God. We do not rule our own lives. God rules in our hearts. Belief implies faith. We rely on God's righteousness and action, not our strength and cunning.

The kingdom is like . . .

Jesus used many familiar illustrations to explain the kingdom. In one parable he told his listeners that the kingdom could be compared with a man who sowed good seed, but an enemy came, sowed weeds, and went away. Later when the weeds grew up among the wheat, the owner was told of the situation. "An enemy has done this," he concludes. His workers ask if they should weed the field. "No," says the owner, "for in gathering the weeds you would uproot the wheat along with them" (see MATTHEW 13:24-30). No doubt Jesus was answering those who wanted to know why, if God was in charge, something hadn't been done about the condition of the world.

A mustard seed

Jesus also compared the kingdom with a mustard seed. Although a small seed, it grows into a good-sized tree in which birds can nest. Perhaps Jesus was remembering Ezekiel 31 in which Assyria is described as a tree that towered above the other trees, in whose branches the birds of the air made their nests. Such a figure of speech—comparing a nation or empire to a great tree with all its branches—was common in Jesus' time. His listeners would readily understand that the illustration described the kingdom, reaching out in every direction and growing to significant dimensions.

Yeast

Jesus referred to the kingdom as yeast. The action of yeast was well known to his listeners. Again they would think in terms of growth. Jesus referred to the kingdom as a treasure hidden in a field (there were no banks, so it was a common practice to bury one's wealth for safekeeping) which someone found and then hid again so that he could sell all he had to buy the field. Jesus compared the kingdom with a pearl merchant who, having found a pearl of great value, sold all the rest in order to obtain just that one. "Have you understood all this?" he asked his disciples (MATTHEW 13:51) and they all claimed that they had.

The kingdom is yours

In his sermon on the mount, Jesus taught that the poor in spirit will be truly happy because the kingdom of heaven is theirs. The poor in spirit are those who have no power or influence. Though they are without prestige on earth, they are truly happy because they can trust God. They know that in the eyes of God each one is important. The hairs of their head are numbered (see MATTHEW 10:30; LUKE 12:7). If God cares for the birds of air and knows when a sparrow falls (MATTHEW 10:29; Luke 12:6), how much more is God concerned for his children? In the same sermon, Jesus said, "Strive first for the kingdom of God and his righteousness, and all [the necessities of life] will be given to you as well" (MATTHEW 6:33).

On one occasion the disciples tried to prevent some parents, who were bringing their children to be blessed, from disturbing Jesus. "But when Jesus saw this," says Mark, "he was indignant and said to [the disciples], 'Let the little children come to me; do not stop them; for it is to such as these that the kingdom of God belongs. Truly I tell you, whoever does not receive the kingdom of God as a little child will never enter it.' And he took them up in his arms, laid his hands on them, and blessed them" (MARK 10:14-16).

When the disciples asked that Jesus teach them to pray, one of the petitions in Jesus' prayer asked God to bring about the kingdom. Each time we pray the Lord's Prayer we say "your kingdom come, your will be done, on earth as in heaven." These are parallel phrases. It was common for the Jews to make a statement and follow it with a second which said essentially the same as the first, or amplified the first. This means that God's kingdom comes when God's will is done on earth, just as we believe God's will is certainly done in heaven.

A simple request

James and John came to Jesus with a request. These were the two disciples who, together with Peter, were witnesses of Jesus' transfiguration. "Teacher," they began, "we want you to do for us whatever we ask of you." That must have put Jesus on his guard! When someone asks, "Will you do me a favor?" it is wise to reply, "First, tell me the favor and then I'll tell you whether or not I'll do it." "What is it?" asked Jesus. They replied, "Grant us to sit, one at your right hand and one at your left, in your glory" (MARK 10:35-37). Later, at the time of his crucifixion, one of the criminals hanging by his side asked Jesus to be remembered when Jesus came into his kingdom. James and John asked for essentially the same thing, but claimed for themselves positions of power and prestige. "You do not know what you are asking," said Jesus. "Are you able to drink the cup that I drink, or be baptized with the baptism that I am baptized with?" They both responded, "Yes, we are able." Then Jesus said to them, "The cup that I drink you will drink; and with the baptism with which I am baptized, you will be baptized; but to sit at my right hand or at my left is not mine to grant . . ." (see MARK 10:38-40).

King of the Jews

When the Wise Men came seeking Jesus, they asked "Where is the child who has been born king of the Jews? For we observed his star at its rising, and have come to pay him homage" (MATTHEW 2:2). From the time of his birth, the idea surfaced that Jesus was some kind of earthly ruler. It continued, as we have seen, until his death. Only in retrospect did the disciples and the early church finally recognize the true dimension and meaning of the kingdom of God.

The foregoing passages help faithful followers of Jesus understand what it means to seek first the kingdom of God and the righteousness of God. Christian stewards will, constantly and consistently, seek to know and do God's will in all things. To be faithful is to want to do that which is pleasing to God.

QUESTIONS FOR REFLECTION

1. What does it mean to you to "seek first the kingdom of God"? How does this help you to be a faithful steward?

2. When you pray the Lord's Prayer, how does praying for the coming of God's kingdom relate to your stewardship? Does your stewardship help the kingdom to come?

3. Jesus referred to the kingdom and also to faith in terms of a mustard seed. How are these two ideas related? How does this relationship help us to be faithful stewards?

9
AND THE WINNER IS . . .

Satan thinks he has won

The Passover was at hand. Mark tells us that "the chief priests and the scribes were looking for a way to arrest Jesus by stealth and kill him; for they said, 'Not during the festival, or there may be a riot among the people'" (MARK 14:1-2).

Jesus had made arrangements for a place where he and his disciples could share the Passover meal. When evening came they went to the house and gathered in the upstairs room. Mark says, "While they were eating, he took a loaf of bread, and after blessing it he broke it, gave it to them, and said, 'Take; this is my body.' Then he took a cup, and after giving thanks he gave it to them, and all of them drank from it. He said to them, 'This is my blood of the covenant, which is poured out for many. Truly I tell you, I will never again drink of the fruit of the vine until that day when I drink it new in the kingdom of God'" (MARK 14:22-25).

The central act of worship

At the time, the disciples probably did not think of this meal as all that different or special. However, in retrospect, after the events that were about to take place, this meal became the central focus of their time together.

Jesus knew they would be confused and afraid, but throughout this meal of bread and wine he would be present in their midst. The meal became that which sustained them in their mission. It is the same for us as Christian stewards today. Holy Communion provides what we need to continue ministering in Christ's name in God's world. Every time we commune, we recall and, in a sense, reenact the events of that first Maundy Thursday. Through Holy Communion we are forgiven and strengthened for our task as stewards.

Matthew, Mark, and Luke all continue to tell the story in a similar way, although there are minor differences. We will use Mark's version as the basis for our consideration.

The time is getting short

Following the meal, Jesus and his disciples went to the Mount of Olives. Jesus told them: "You will all become deserters" (MARK 14:26). Peter, again the first to speak up, said: "You can count on me! Even if everybody else deserts you, I never will" (see MARK 14:29). Jesus, still patient with Peter, said, "Truly I tell you, this day, this very night, before the cock crows twice, you will deny me three times" (MARK 14:30). But Peter needed to make his point. "Even if I have to give my life, I'm not going to be the one who denies you" (see MARK 14:31). Mark tells us that all the disciples said virtually the same thing. You can see them in your mind's eye, standing in the background saying such things as "Here, here!" "You can count on me!" "I'll never desert you!"

Stay awake!

Jesus and the disciples then went to Gethsemane where he wanted to pray. "Sit here," he told the whole group and then took Peter, James, and John with him and told them, "I am deeply grieved, even to death; remain here, and keep awake" (MARK 14:34). It sounded good in theory, and no doubt the disciples had great resolve, but they just could not stay awake. Three times Jesus found them sleeping. How exasperating that must have been. He was facing the most extreme test of his whole life. It was something he would rather not face. Could it be still another temptation? Had Satan found another "opportune time"? "Abba," he began his prayer, using an Aramaic child's term for father. "Father, for you all things are possible; remove this cup from me; yet, not what I want, but what you want" (MARK 14:36).

He returned to his disciples only to find them asleep. "Are you still sleeping?" he asked them the third time. "The hour has come," he said, "the Son of Man is betrayed into the hands of sinners. Get up, let us be going. See, my betrayer is at hand" (MARK 14:41-42).

The hour has come!

It was one of the twelve, Judas Iscariot, who arrived with an armed crowd to arrest Jesus. A scuffle ensued and in the melee, a slave of the high priest was wounded. Jesus tried to restore order: "Have you come out with swords and clubs to arrest me as though I were a bandit?" he asked. "Day after day I was with you in the temple teaching, and you did not arrest me. But let the scriptures be fulfilled" (MARK 14:48-49). He was referring to Zechariah 13 (see MARK 14:27).

It is at this point that events are too stressful for the disciples. Mark puts it matter-of-factly: "*All* of them deserted him and fled" (MARK 14:50, italics added).

Peter denies his Lord

Jesus was taken to the authorities to be judged. They couldn't really prove their charges. Mark said, "Many gave false testimony" (14:56). Peter, a deserter, waited near the fire in the courtyard trying to get warm. A servant girl of the high priest saw him, pointed and said, "You also were with Jesus, the man from Nazareth." But Peter denied it. And suddenly, in the background, the cock crowed. The servant girl turned to the others in the courtyard. "This man is one of them I tell you." But Peter denied it. The bystanders weren't so sure. "You are one of them," they said. "You are a Galilean." But Peter began to curse and swore that he did not know Jesus. The cock crowed a second time and Peter remembered what Jesus had said. Peter broke down and began to sob (see MARK 14:66-72).

Meanwhile, those holding Jesus were mocking and beating him. "Prophesy!" they taunted him. "Who is it that struck you?" (LUKE 22:63).

The next day

"When morning came," says Matthew, "all the chief priests and the elders of the people conferred together against Jesus in order to bring about his death" (MATTHEW 27:1). "If you are the Messiah, tell us," they said. "If I tell you," replied Jesus, "you will not believe; and if I question you, you will not answer. But from now on the Son of Man will be seated at the right hand of the power of God" (LUKE 22:67-69).

The secret is out!

This is what Jesus was discussing with Moses and Elijah at the time of his transfiguration (see chapter 7). This was what he warned his disciples not to reveal. Now Jesus had made it plain. "Are you, then, the Son of God?" they all asked (LUKE 22:70a). Jesus' reply was straightforward. Using a polite Jewish form of speech, he said in effect, "Yes, I am." (See LUKE 22:70b.) "What further testimony do we need?" they all asked. "We have heard it ourselves from his own lips!" (LUKE 22:71). Matthew says simply, "They bound him, led him away, and handed him over to Pilate the governor" (MATTHEW 27:2).

What is truth?

Pilate's basic question to Jesus was: "Are you the King of the Jews?" (JOHN 18:33b; MATTHEW 27:11; Mark 15:2; LUKE 23:3). Many people, from the Wise Men to Pilate, linked Jesus with the concept of kingship. Pilate's question also suggested the charge against Jesus—that he was a revolutionary. It was a charge for which the punishment was execution.

Jesus replied: "Do you ask this on your own, or did others tell you about me?" Pilate answered with another question: "I am not a Jew, am I? Your own nation and the chief priests have handed you over to me. What have you done?" Jesus answered, "My kingdom is not from this world. If my kingdom were from this world, my followers would be fighting to keep me from being handed over to the Jews. But as it is, my kingdom is not from here." We can hear the note of triumph in Pilate's exclamation: "So you are a king?" Pilate believed he had proved his point! "You say that I am a king," replied Jesus, meaning for all intents and purposes, "Yes." "For this I was born," continued Jesus, "and for this I came into the world, to testify to the truth. Everyone who belongs to the truth listens to my voice." Pilate became annoyed and asked him, "What is truth?" (JOHN 18:34-38).

Barabbas, not Jesus

Then Pilate told those who had brought Jesus to him that he found no case against him. They didn't want to hear that. They had come with a certain purpose, and they wanted it carried out. Pilate tried another tack: "But you have a custom that I release someone for you at the Passover. Do you want me to release for you the King of the Jews?" They shouted, "Not this man, but Barabbas!" (JOHN 18:39-40).

Those who had hailed Jesus on the occasion of his triumphal entry into Jerusalem just five days earlier, were now calling for his death. They wanted Barabbas. Why? Because Barabbas was a proven revolutionary. They had believed Judas when he told them that Jesus would lead the revolt. But all Jesus had done since Sunday was stir things up by overturning the tables of the moneychangers in the Temple and speaking out against the status quo.

Pilate ordered Jesus to be flogged. The soldiers assigned to this task decided to have some sport with him. They wove a crown of thorns, dressed him in a royal robe, and paid him "homage" by slapping his face.

"Crucify him! Crucify him!"

Pilate tried once more. "Look," he said, "I am bringing him out to you to let you know that I find no case against him"

(JOHN 19:4). But by now the crowd had been stirred up, probably by those same zealots who stirred them up on the first day of the week. "Crucify him! Crucify him!" they cried. "Do it yourselves," said Pilate in disgust. They knew, of course, that under Roman law they couldn't; only Pilate could. "We have a law," they said, "and according to that law he ought to die because he has claimed to be the Son of God" (JOHN 19:7).

Pilate began to see the seriousness of the situation. Recognizing that he might be caught in the middle, he went to Jesus and said, "Who are you really? Where do you really come from?" (see JOHN 19:9). Jesus didn't say a word. "Do you refuse to speak to me?" Pilate said. "Do you not know that I have power to release you, and the power to crucify you?" Jesus answered, "You would have no power over me unless it had been given you from above" (JOHN 19:10-11a).

One more time . . .

Pilate tried again to release Jesus, but the crowd would not listen. "If you release this man," they threatened, "you are no friend of the emperor. Everyone who claims to be a king sets himself against the emperor" (JOHN 19:12). These were the people who had hailed Jesus as king on the previous Sunday. Some of them might even have been in the crowd of five thousand who wanted to make him king after his miraculous feeding of them. But here they had another purpose and they knew Pilate could not refuse. He would be risking his whole career—a career that already had some marks against it. Pilate dared not allow the emperor to hear that he was disloyal or wavering in his duty.

Reluctantly, Pilate ordered the crucifixion of Jesus and put an inscription on the cross to indicate the charge upon which he was being executed. John reports, "It read, 'Jesus of Nazareth, the King of the Jews.' Many of the Jews read this inscription, because the place where Jesus was crucified was near the city; and it was written in Hebrew, in Latin, and in Greek. Then the chief priests of the Jews said to Pilate, 'Do not write, "The King of the Jews," but "This man said, I am

King of the Jews.'" Pilate answered angrily, 'What I have written, I have written'" (JOHN 19:19-22).

Today you will be with me in Paradise

Two others—common criminals—were crucified that day. One of them derided Jesus: "Are you not the Messiah? Save yourself and us!" (LUKE 23:39). The other rebuked him and reminded him that they were being punished for what they had done, observing that Jesus was not guilty of anything (LUKE 23:40-41). It is the fourth time this point is made by Luke (see LUKE 23:4, 14, 22), and will be made again (see LUKE 23:47). The man said to Jesus: "Remember me when you come into your kingdom." Jesus replied: "Truly I tell you, today you will be with me in Paradise" (LUKE 23:42-43).

It is over . . .

"When it was noon," says Mark, "darkness came over the whole land until three in the afternoon" (MARK 15:33). Each of the gospel writers has his own way of telling the story, each supplying various accounts of what Jesus said while on the cross. Matthew, Luke, and Mark all tell us that at the end, in Mark's words, "Jesus gave a loud cry and breathed his last" (MARK 15:37; MATTHEW 27:50; LUKE 23:46). John says simply, "Then he bowed his head and gave up his spirit" (JOHN 19:30).

Jesus was taken down from the cross, but it was late in the day. Little could be done to make the usual preparations for burial, because the Sabbath was rapidly approaching and Jewish law was very specific about what could or could not be done on the Sabbath.

All the gospel writers report that a man named Joseph, who was from Arimathea, went to Pilate and asked for the body of Jesus. He wrapped the body in linen and placed it in a tomb. Luke's report is simple and straightforward (see LUKE 23:50-56). John adds more detail, indicating that "Nicodemus, who had at first come to Jesus by night, also came" (JOHN 19:39). Mark and Matthew report that Joseph rolled a stone against the door of the tomb (see MARK 15:46; MATTHEW 27:60). Only

Matthew reports that Pilate sent soldiers to guard the tomb for fear that the disciples would come, steal the body, and claim that Jesus had risen from the dead. As a further precaution, the soldiers sealed the stone to the entrance of the tomb (see MATTHEW 27:62-66).

For all intents and purposes, it seems that the story of Jesus is complete, his mission has ended in failure. Satan appears to be the victor. Death has put an end to whatever it was that Jesus was trying to do.

But God is preparing a surprise . . .

QUESTIONS FOR REFLECTION

1. Do you receive Holy Communion on a regular basis? How does an understanding of this sacrament as our central act of worship inform your Christian stewardship?

2. Peter denied Jesus by claiming that he was not one of his disciples. What are some of the ways—subtle and not so subtle—that we deny Jesus?

3. Sometimes as we look at our world of hunger, war, tragedy, and defenselessness, it would appear that evil has overcome good. Yet the cross of Christ gives hope to faithful stewards. How does this affect the way you live?

10
THE VICTORY
OF CHRIST

Satan loses . . . for all time!

It was Sunday morning, the first day of the week. The women were the first to go to the tomb. They wanted to properly prepare the body of Jesus. As they went, they wondered to themselves, "Who will roll away the stone for us from the entrance to the tomb?" (MARK 16:3).

Mark, Luke, and John all report simply that the stone was rolled away, but Matthew attributes it to "a great earthquake; for an angel of the Lord, descending from heaven, came and rolled back the stone and sat on it" (MATTHEW 28:2). In Matthew's account, this angel was the one who told them that Jesus had risen (see MATTHEW 28:6). Luke speaks of "two men in dazzling clothes" who stood beside them and told them about Jesus (see LUKE 24:4). According to Mark (16:5-6), they entered the tomb to receive the news. In John's account, it was only Mary Magdalene who went to the tomb, and upon seeing the stone rolled away, immediately ran to "Peter and the other disciple, the one whom Jesus loved, and said to them, 'They have taken the Lord out of the tomb, and we do not know where they have laid him'" (JOHN 20:2). This set the stage for Peter and "the other disciple" to run to the tomb. Peter lost the race, but was the first to enter the tomb. He found nothing but the linen wrappings that had once covered Jesus' body. John's description of the scene suggests that Jesus simply stepped out of the grave clothes and walked away (see John 20:6-7).

Jesus is alive!

All the gospel accounts agree that it was not the empty tomb that convinced his followers that Jesus had risen from the dead, but the words of the angels (see MATTHEW 28:5-7; Mark 16:6-7; LUKE 24:5-9) and, in John's account, a series of encounters with the risen Lord. Matthew and Mark mention these post-resurrection appearances but give little detail. Luke tells the story of two of Jesus' followers who encounter him on the road to the village of Emmaus, and subsequently return to Jerusalem. They reported that Jesus suddenly appeared in their midst, explained to them what had happened, and commissioned them to continue his ministry. Luke ends with a brief account of the ascension (see LUKE 24:13-52).

It is John who by far has the most detail about the post-resurrection appearances of Jesus. Many scholars believe that John's last chapter (21) is not part of the original manuscript. Even without that chapter, John relies heavily on Jesus' appearances in the upper room to confirm the fact of the resurrection.

First, we have the story of Mary Magdalene, standing outside the tomb. She met Jesus but did not immediately recognize him, thinking he was the gardener (see JOHN 20:11-18).

Next, John tells of the encounter between Jesus and one of the disciples whom we have come to call "Doubting Thomas," a name that actually misses the point of the story. Thomas might have doubted at first, but ultimately he believed and became a man of great faith, recognizing Jesus not only as Lord, but also God. Let's look at the story in detail.

It was evening and the disciples were gathered in the upper room for fear of the authorities. They believed that if Jesus could be arrested and put to death, so might they. They had locked the door, but that did not prevent Jesus from entering. Suddenly he was standing in their midst. You can almost see and feel the fright of the disciples. "Peace be with you," said Jesus (JOHN 20:19b). In Hebrew the word for peace is *shalom*. It means more than the absence of fear or turmoil; rather it refers to everything that makes life wholesome, enjoyable, and positive. Shalom is a good word for Christian stewards.

"After he said this," reports John, "[Jesus] showed them his hands and his side. Then the disciples rejoiced when they saw the Lord. Jesus said to them again, 'Peace be with you. As the Father has sent me, so I send you.' When he had said this, he breathed on them and said to them, 'Receive the Holy Spirit. If you forgive the sins of any, they are forgiven them; if you retain the sins of any, they are retained'" (JOHN 20:20-23). Luke tells the story differently as we shall see in Chapter 13. For Luke, the disciples undergo a dramatic change in full, public view, whereas in John, the experience is in the privacy of the upper room after Jesus and his disciples had eaten the last supper. The words about forgiveness are kingdom words, as in Matthew, when Jesus changed Simon's name to Peter and said to him: "I will give you the keys of the kingdom of heaven, and whatever you bind on earth will be bound in heaven, and whatever you loose on earth will be loosed in heaven" (MATTHEW 16:19). In Matthew's account, it would appear that Peter received this power alone. In John's version it is clear that Jesus intended it to be for all the disciples.

The following week

Thomas was not in the upper room when Jesus appeared to the disciples. Where he was is unclear. Perhaps like other followers of Jesus, he decided to leave Jerusalem for a while to escape the clutches of the authorities. Perhaps he thought it foolish of the other disciples to hide in the upper room. We don't know. All we know is that he came back. The other disciples immediately told him, "We have seen the Lord." Thomas must have wondered if being shut up as they were in a small and cramped room had somehow affected their minds. He wasn't about to buy the story. "Don't expect me to believe," he said, "unless I see the nail marks in his hands and touch the wound in his side."

A week went by. The disciples were still hiding. The doors were shut. Jesus came into their midst and said again: "Peace be with you." Then he turned to Thomas and, with a look of understanding, said: "Here, touch my hands and sides. There is no need for you to doubt. I want you to believe." That was

enough for Thomas. He didn't need anything but Jesus. "My
Lord and my God!" Thomas cried out. (See JOHN 20:24-28.)

The focus of faith

The resurrection became the cornerstone of the Christian faith.
As the Passover is the lens through which the Jews have always
understood their faith, so the cross and resurrection are the
keys to understanding the Christian faith. The disciples suddenly changed. Whereas they had been frightened to the point
of hiding in the upper room behind a locked door for fear of
the authorities, now they flung open that door, and went out,
and turned the world upside down (see ACTS 17:6).

There are several lessons we can learn from this. The early
Christians were so motivated by the resurrection experience
that they began to observe Sunday as the Lord's Day. While
many continued to observe the Sabbath (Saturday) because
they were still faithful to their Jewish heritage, Sunday became
a special day to remember Jesus.

Although the early Christians gathered for worship, they
understood that their mission was not to stay closeted in the
upper room. We often talk about "going to church" and certainly that is desirable and commendable. But we should also
talk about "going from" church. This reflects the pattern Jesus
shared with his disciples: pray, serve, pray, serve. It is important
to worship, but it is also essential to take action. Perhaps we
can describe the pattern in this way: worship, work, worship,
work.

Jesus was often criticized by the religious authorities for
attitudes and actions which they thought to be wrong. On a
certain Sabbath, Jesus and his disciples were going through
the fields, picking and eating ears of corn. The Pharisees were
outraged, not because the disciples were plucking and eating
corn (that was permissible any weekday—see DEUTERONOMY
23:25), but because they were doing it on the Sabbath. Work
on the Sabbath was forbidden, and what they were doing was
classified as work. Thus, in the eyes of the Pharisees, Jesus and
his disciples were breaking the law. For the Pharisees this was
a sin. It was no small thing; it was a matter of life and death

to them. Jesus, however, saw it differently. He reminded his critics of an incident from Jewish history in which David, fleeing for his life, ate holy bread which was reserved only for the priests. It was an unlawful act, but Jesus cited it from Scripture as an example that human need may be more important than religious doctrine and practice. "The sabbath was made for humankind, and not humankind for the sabbath," he told them and added, "so the Son of Man is lord even of the sabbath" (MARK 2:27-28).

Two important lessons

This incident sheds light on two things. First, it helps us to recognize that the church was created for people and not the other way around. So often it seems that the chief reason people are asked to join a congregation is to support the budget and help keep the building clean and the program rolling smoothly along.

Second, it may be that Jesus, remembering the twelve loaves of the Bread of the Presence as an offering to God, turned the concept around and offered the bread to his disciples (and us). Indeed, there may be no better lesson in Christian stewardship than that of Holy Communion. God gives us, in the first place, grain and grape. We take them and change them into bread and wine. The bread and wine are offered as symbols of our stewardship of God's gifts. Then these gifts of bread and wine are blessed by God and given back to us as the body and blood of Christ our Lord. Each time we commune, we do it in response to Jesus' command to remember his death. We should also remember each time we commune that we are stewards, and that our lives are dedicated to serving in the name of Jesus.

What is really important?

Theodore Wedel, in his book *The Gospel in a Strange New World* ([Philadelphia: Westminster Press, 1973], 78–79) tells of a coast guard station that had stood on a dangerous coast for centuries. Before long, the rescue personnel found that they did not spend all their time saving drowning people from shipwrecks, so they devoted their energies to beautifying the station. Soon this became an all encompassing, highly desirable pursuit. The rescue service was largely ignored, but the various drills and rituals were carefully preserved. The actual launching out to rescue people became a profession for which a few were hired and paid. Soon the custodians of the station became upset when the rescuers would bring in persons who were alien, or of a different color, of foreign speech, or maimed from their bout with the sea. "Will they not," so they were tempted to exclaim, "soil the linen on our clean beds, and, moved by gratitude for their rescue, desire to become lifesavers themselves and thus presume to belong by right to our intimate fellowship? Should we not set up a minimum entrance requirement for cleanliness and good manners before we offer shelter? Perhaps we might urge them to build a lifesaving station of their own at a decorous distance from ours."

This striking illustration brings home to us the fact that the church is created for—and should be maintained for—people. To make people the servants of the church is akin to the pharisaical demands related to the Sabbath. In one sense, the congregation exists to welcome those who have yet to come. This sounds very much like what we usually call evangelism. It is. Faithful stewards are also evangelists. As all Christians are called to be stewards, so we are also called to be witnesses. The good news is something we dare not hold back. We share it with all.

Every person is important and of great value

One time the Pharisees and scribes were grumbling about the undesirable people such as tax collectors and prostitutes who came to listen to Jesus. Upright religious people, thought the Pharisees and scribes, should have nothing to do with such rabble. So Jesus posed a question for them: "Which one of you, having a hundred sheep and losing one of them, does not leave the ninety-nine in the wilderness and go after the one that is lost until he finds it? When he has found it, he lays it on his shoulders and rejoices. And when he comes home, he calls together his friends and neighbors, saying to them,

'Rejoice with me, for I have found my sheep that was lost.' Just so, I tell you, there will be more joy in heaven over one sinner who repents than over ninety-nine righteous persons who need no repentance" (LUKE 15:3-7).

Jesus taught that each individual is important. "What woman," he said, "having ten silver coins, if she loses one of them, does not light a lamp, sweep the house, and search carefully until she finds it? When she has found it, she calls together her friends and neighbors, saying, 'Rejoice with me, for I have found the coin that I had lost.' Just so, I tell you, there is joy in the presence of the angels of God over one sinner who repents" (LUKE 15:8-10).

Are these parables about stewardship or evangelism? Actually, both—and more. They are illustrations of God's love—indications of how God loves us. They illustrate the good news that motivates faithful followers of Jesus to witness and serve.

As stewards, we go from the church in peace to proclaim peace. Having received the good news, we serve in the freedom which the gospel of Jesus Christ gives to us. Inspired and empowered by the Holy Spirit, we reach out in love. As the resurrection gave the disciples a new start, so it gives us new life and energy to manage and use all the gifts that God has given and continues to give us.

QUESTIONS FOR REFLECTION

1. The disciples are greatly changed by their experience of the resurrection of their Lord. How does the Easter message speak to you as a faithful steward?

2. If the church is created for people—and not people for the church—what does this say about Christian stewardship?

3. The story of the coast guard station teaches us a very important lesson about priorities. As a Christian steward, what are the priorities in your life?

4. Sometimes it is difficult to distinguish between evangelism and stewardship. How are they different? How are they alike? What do the answers say to Christian stewards?

11
FEED MY SHEEP

Faithful followers take action

The events of Good Friday and Easter Sunday were past, and a group of Jesus' disciples had gathered at the Sea of Tiberias. Peter told the others, "I am going fishing" (JOHN 21:3). What else was there to do? The others decided to go along. Did this mean they had decided to return to their old trade? Did they think that their three-year adventure with Jesus was over and now it was time to return to their former occupations?

John tells us, "just after daybreak, Jesus stood on the beach; but the disciples did not know that it was Jesus" (JOHN 21:4). Jesus observed that they had not caught any fish and told them to cast the net on the other side of the boat. When they did, they were unable to haul in the net because the catch was so huge. Suddenly one of them—John calls him "that disciple whom Jesus loved"—said to Peter: "It is the Lord!" (JOHN 21:7). Peter jumped out of the boat and headed for shore, leaving the others to follow in the boat, dragging with them the net full of fish.

When they came ashore, they saw a charcoal fire with fish on it, and some bread. Jesus asked for some of the fish they had just caught. Peter fetched them and Jesus said: "Come and have breakfast" (JOHN 21:12).

When the meal was over, Jesus quizzed Peter. "Simon son of John," he said, "do you love me more than these?" Peter answered, "Yes, Lord; you know that I love you." "Feed my lambs," said Jesus. Then a second time Jesus asked Peter: "Simon, son of John, do you love me?" Peter, with emphasis replied: "Yes, Lord; you know that I love you." "Tend my sheep," said Jesus. A third time Jesus asked the question, and by now Peter felt a little hurt. "Lord," he said, "you know everything; and especially you know that I love you!" "Feed my sheep," said Jesus (see JOHN 21:15-19).

Jesus speaks to us

The words of the resurrected Jesus to Peter are also addressed to contemporary Christian stewards. Now we are the ones who are faced with that question, and we are the ones who must answer. To each of us our Lord asks, "Do you love me?" The question is as personal as that. It is addressed to each one of us just as it was addressed to Peter, not the group of disciples in general. And the answer must come from each one of us, as well.

It is a persistent question. Jesus does not ask it once and never again, just as temptation does not simply come once and then disappear forever. The persistence of the question points to the fact that throughout our lives there is the ever-present danger of being lured away from our mission by Satan. As stewards, we need regularly to affirm our faith and commit ourselves to the mission given us by our Lord.

Our chief shepherd

There are many references to sheep and shepherds in the New Testament. Jesus described himself as the Good Shepherd (JOHN 10:1-16). This passage is often used at the installation of a pastor. It speaks also to faithful stewards who are engaged in the mission and ministry they are called to perform. The early church referred to Jesus as the "great shepherd of the sheep" (HEBREWS 13:20) and the "chief shepherd" (1 PETER 5:4).

In the Old Testament there are frequent references to God as shepherd and the people as God's flock. Perhaps the best known and most loved is Psalm 23: "The Lord is my shepherd." Nor is it unusual for this metaphor to be applied to kings and priests of God. This is probably because it would be readily understood by people who were, for the most part, nomadic shepherds. King David, for example, was a shepherd as a boy and later shepherd of the people as king.

The shepherd metaphor is apt. Shepherding was a full-time job. No shepherd went off duty except for the most important reasons. We often miss this when we are told in the Christmas story that the shepherds, when they heard of the Messiah's birth, decided that they must hurry to Bethlehem. It meant that this event was of vital importance. Otherwise, nothing would have taken them away from their flocks.

The life of a shepherd was not easy. In fact, it was downright dangerous, especially because wild animals tried to attack the flocks. Yet the sheep were safe when the shepherd was near. "Even though I walk through the darkest valley, I fear no evil; for you are with me; your rod and your staff—they comfort me" (PSALM 23:4). The shepherd's rod—what we call a *crook*—was used to snare sheep that were straying and to pull them back. The shepherd's *staff* was a short club for beating off marauding animals and robbers. A lamb might well feel secure when defended by such a shepherd. You and I know security in the presence of our Good Shepherd.

Grass was not always readily available, and sheep had a way of wandering off in search of food. They had to be constantly watched. The terrain itself was often dangerous. Sheep might fall and injure themselves—or worse. Without a shepherd they were in trouble.

The Good Shepherd

It is worth examining what the New Testament tells us about Jesus as shepherd. Mark tells us that just before feeding the five thousand, Jesus looked at all those people "and he had compassion for them, because they were like sheep without a shepherd" (MARK 6:34). Jesus understood his mission to be the seeking of "the lost sheep of the house of Israel" (MATTHEW 15:24). He wanted to bring them back, even if it meant one by one, just as a shepherd would expend the time and energy to seek one lost lamb (see LUKE 15:3-7).

John may be the most helpful in considering Jesus as the Good Shepherd. He quotes Jesus:

> I am the good shepherd. The good shepherd lays down his life for the sheep. The hired hand, who is not the shepherd and does not own the sheep, sees the wolf coming and leaves the sheep and runs away—and the wolf snatches them and scatters them. The hired hand runs away because a hired hand does not care for the sheep. I am the good shepherd. I know my own and my own know me, just as the Father knows me and I know the Father. And I lay down my life for the sheep" (JOHN 10:11-15).

On one occasion, Jesus was preaching to a large crowd when someone wanted his help. "Teacher," the man called out, "tell my brother to divide the family inheritance with me." Jesus' first reaction was one of surprise. "Friend, who set me to be a judge or arbitrator over you?" (LUKE 12:13-14). This event prompted Jesus to begin teaching a number of parables about stewardship, the first to the crowd and the rest to his disciples. All of this is for those of us who are called to be stewards.

A warning

"Take care!" he began. "Be on your guard against all kinds of greed; for one's life does not consist in the abundance of possessions" (LUKE 12:15). And he told them a parable about a rich man who was fortunate enough to have a crop so large that he could not store it all in his barns. What should he do? Jesus didn't give all the options, but the man might have thought of several schemes—selling the grain, giving it away— but he finally decided to tear down his present buildings and erect larger ones to hold his crops and all of his possessions. The man felt good about his decision. "And I will say to my soul, 'Soul, you have ample goods laid up for many years; relax, eat, drink, be merry'" (LUKE 12:19). But God had a surprise in Jesus' parable. "You fool!" said God. "This very night your life is being demanded of you. And the things you have pre-pared, whose will they be?" (LUKE 12:20). Jesus summed it up by saying: "So it is with those who store up treasures for themselves but are not rich toward God" (LUKE 12:21).

Good advice

Later, Jesus said to his disciples, "Do not worry about your life, what you will eat, or about your body, what you will wear. For life is more than food, and the body more than clothing" (LUKE 12:22). "Instead, strive for [God's] kingdom, and these things will be given to you as well. Do not be afraid, little flock, for it is your Father's good pleasure to give you the kingdom" (LUKE 12:31-32). This is kingdom language and shepherd language rolled into one illustration.

Words to live by

"Sell your possessions," Jesus continued, "and give alms. Make purses for yourselves that do not wear out, an unfailing treasure in heaven, where no thief comes near and no moth destroys. For where your treasure is, there your heart will be also" (LUKE 12:33-34). This teaching of Jesus is often used by preachers to talk about giving money, and the sermons usually distort what Jesus was saying. Emphasis on money and material pos-sessions ties us to this world. The old phrase, "You can't take it with you," is not only true; it points up the real problem. Money is of this world. Jesus was talking about a treasure in heaven "where neither moth nor rust consumes and where thieves do not break in and steal" (MATTHEW 6:20). When Jesus said that it is more difficult for a rich man to enter heaven than a camel to go through the eye of a needle (MATTHEW 19:24; MARK 10:25; LUKE 18:25), he was pointing out that material possessions make it difficult to want to leave this earth, and even more difficult to fix one's sights on eternity. Because faithful stewards know where their true treasure is, they are able to keep things in focus. Christian stewards know what is important and what is not. They have their priorities straight.

Money

Money, of course, makes mission possible. The gas company does not accept pious statements as a substitute for payment of the monthly bill. No matter how dedicated and committed our pastors are, they cannot feed and clothe their families without money. The mission of the church, whether local, regional, national, or international, requires money. It is important to support the mission of the church, but it is even more important to know why we are providing that support. If it is only to pay bills that will keep the church doors open and the pastor in the pulpit, we may miss the true joy of giving. But when we recognize how God has blessed us, and that our giving is a response to what we have first been given, everything falls into perspective.

Stewards as managers

Tithers have long recognized that they are managers of all their money, not just the ten percent given to the work of the Lord through the congregation. That is ten percent set aside or, to put it another way, taken "off the top." It is, in an old phrase, "first-fruits giving."

Many who do not tithe wonder how anyone can give ten percent of personal income and still pay all the bills. The answer is quite simple. To tithe is to be deliberate. It is to plan. And when you know how the first ten percent will be used, it is quite easy to decide how to use the other ninety percent.

A pledge is a faith commitment

Many church members question the practice of pledging. Some may even be proud of their refusal to pledge. Often they say that they cannot make such a commitment because they don't know what the future holds. Such an attitude is sad, because it means that they have little faith that God will provide for them. "Consider the ravens" said Jesus; "they neither sow nor reap, they have neither storehouse nor barn, and yet God feeds them. . . . Consider the lilies, how they grow: they neither toil nor spin; yet I tell you, even Solomon in all his glory was not clothed like one of these. But if God so clothes the grass of the field, which is alive today and tomorrow is thrown into the oven, how much more will he clothe you—you of little faith!" (LUKE 12:24, 27-28).

To pledge, to give, to tithe—all these are acts of faith. Faithful followers of Jesus respond to God's call and God's blessings by living lives of witness and service. Jesus asks each of us, as he asked Peter, "Do you love me?" When we answer "yes," he tells us what he told Peter and the rest of the disciples: "Feed my sheep."

QUESTIONS FOR REFLECTION

1. What does it mean for us in our time to feed the sheep and lambs of Jesus? Where does this happen? When does it happen?

2. Can we take Jesus literally when he says "Do not worry about your life" and "Sell your possessions?" Or is there a deeper meaning? What is it? How does it make us more faithful stewards?

3. Are you a tither? Do you pledge? How can such disciplines increase the faithfulness of a Christian steward?

12
GO, MAKE DISCIPLES

Our mission is universal

The time has come for Jesus to return and receive his royal welcome into heaven. The action begun with the transfiguration is now concluded with the ascension.

Luke tells us that Jesus led his disciples to Bethany and there "lifting up his hands, he blessed them. While he was blessing them, he withdrew from them and was carried up into heaven. And they worshiped him, and returned to Jerusalem with great joy; and they were continually in the temple blessing God" (LUKE 24:50b-53).

Just before this event, Jesus (according to Luke) told his disciples: "Thus it is written, that the Messiah is to suffer and to rise from the dead on the third day, and that repentance and forgiveness of sins is to be proclaimed in his name to all nations, beginning from Jerusalem. You are witnesses of these things. And see, I am sending upon you what my Father promised; so stay here in the city until you have been clothed with power from on high" (LUKE 24:46-49).

The disciples are commissioned

Luke continues his story in a second volume which we know as the Acts of the Apostles. There he gives additional details concerning the ascension of Jesus, telling us that as the disciples watched, Jesus "was lifted up, and a cloud took him out of their sight. While he was going and they were gazing up toward heaven, suddenly two men in white robes stood by them. They said, 'Men of Galilee, why do you stand looking up toward heaven? This Jesus, who has been taken up from you into heaven, will come in the same way as you saw him go into heaven" (ACTS 1:9b-11).

Matthew sets the scene on a mountain in Galilee where Jesus told his disciples: "All authority in heaven and on earth has been given to me. Go therefore and make disciples of all nations, baptizing them in the name of the Father and of the Son and of the Holy Spirit, and teaching them to obey everything that I have commanded you. And remember, I am with you always, to the end of the age" (MATTHEW 28:18-20).

And so, the mission of Jesus was passed on to the disciples, who would wait to be empowered by the Holy Spirit.

In future years the church will confess in its creeds that Jesus "ascended into heaven, and is seated at the right hand of [God]" (meaning that his authority is recognized in heaven).

We are commissioned

Just as the disciples were commissioned to go, teach, baptize, and make disciples, so this mission is the primary task of the church, even in our own day. You and I, as the modern-day counterparts of the disciples, are called to go, teach, baptize, and make disciples. Where are we to go and whom are we to teach, baptize, and make into disciples? The simple answers are "everywhere" and "everyone."

No waiting

Our mission is an urgent one. At times, we need to be reminded of the question asked by the two angels: "Why do you stand looking up toward heaven?" (ACTS 1:11). Our ministry is here and now on earth with human beings who are hungry, suffering, and in desperate need of hearing the good news of Jesus Christ. It is nice to hang around and fix up the coast guard station, but the tempests that rage in the world and in the lives of people will not allow us that luxury.

In Paul's letter to young Timothy are words that stewards should take to heart: "In the presence of God and of Christ Jesus, who is to judge the living and the dead, and in view of his appearing and his kingdom, I solemnly urge you: proclaim the message; be persistent whether the time is favorable or unfavorable; convince, rebuke, and encourage, with the utmost patience in teaching. . . . As for you, always be sober, endure suffering, do the work of an evangelist,"—for our purposes we could read that *steward*—"carry out your ministry fully" (2 TIMOTHY 4:1-2, 5). The urgency is real; we dare not postpone our stewardship.

Teach

Jesus was called rabbi, or teacher, by friend and foe alike, because for all practical, public purposes he was seen as an itinerant preacher. While some may have used the title out of mere politeness, Jesus' approach was similar, if not identical, to the methods traditionally used by the rabbis of the time. He sat in the synagogues, for example, and commented on Scripture. He had a band of learners (disciples) who accompanied him, listening to his stories and discourse. Teaching was a basic, vital part of his ministry and so, when the disciples took over Jesus' mission, they also made teaching an important part of their work.

The teaching of Jesus, however, was more than the public image and traditional methodology. What he was able to do as teacher—unlike any other rabbi, unlike the disciples, and unlike ourselves—was to make himself the subject of his own teaching. That is, he himself was the fulfillment of much that he taught. And yet, he did not claim authority for his teaching and preaching, but gave all the glory to his Father. "If I testify about myself," he said to those who questioned what he was doing, "my testimony is not true. There is another who testifies on my behalf, and I know that his testimony to me is true" (JOHN 5:31-32). Faithful followers of Jesus never seek glory for themselves or claim any authority except that which is given them by God.

There were times, however, when Jesus was blunt—speaking in words that were straightforward, and not subject to mis-interpretation. "You search the scriptures," he told the religious authorities, "because you think that in them you have eternal life; and it is they that testify on my behalf. Yet you refuse to come to me to have life. I do not accept glory from human beings. But I know that you do not have the love of God in you. I have come in my Father's name, and you do not accept me; if another comes in his own name, you will accept him. How can you believe when you accept glory from one another and do not seek the glory that comes from the one who alone is God? Do not think that I will accuse you before the Father; your accuser is Moses, on whom you have set your hope. If you believed Moses, you would believe me . . ." (JOHN 5:39-46). It was words like this, of course, that ultimately led to Jesus' death. That, however, was a risk he was willing to take. He had decided to serve—and tell the truth—no matter what the cost. Good stewards must, like Jesus, take up their cross and be willing to risk the cost.

There are lessons here for good stewards. What we teach is not based on our own authority, but on God's. Scripture is the basis for our teaching and our stewardship—the norm for faith and life. We teach in love because the very basis for our stewardship and our teaching is love. Love was a central, if not *the* central, theme of the teaching of Jesus.

Teaching and preaching

The early church made a distinction between teaching and preaching. Teaching was based on Scripture and primarily ad-dressed to Jews who already believed in God. The purpose of such teaching was to show how Scripture had been fulfilled in Christ. Preaching, on the other hand, was aimed primarily at those who still needed to be convinced. It soon became clear, however, that once they, too, had become believers, they were in need of teaching and doctrine.

In today's church the distinction between teaching and preaching remains, but because of the composition of the au-dience, the approach is different. Whereas at one time preach-ing was exclusively proclamation, today it must contain ele-ments of teaching to be relevant or even understandable to some persons. The decision to limit sermons to be instruments of proclamation alone and to restrict all teaching to the classroom may have been effective in the past, but in many congregations today such an arrangement simply does not work.

Preaching has become storytelling, which is essentially what Jesus did in his parables. Some preachers make the mistake of thinking that storytelling begins with some personal experience and ends with application of Scripture. This kind of approach might be called "a-funny-thing-happened-to-me-on-the-way-to-church" preaching. It doesn't work for very long. The problem is not that the listeners don't understand. It isn't even that the preachers aren't skillful. It's that there are just so many personal illustrations one can use before running out of them, or sounding egotistical, or, eventually, giving the impression that the stories have been invented.

This is not to say that personal stories and other modern-day examples should not be used in preaching. They should, but, interesting and fresh though they may be, they can never substitute for God's story. The parables of Jesus and the accounts of his preaching, teaching, and miracles should be at the heart of our proclamation and witness.

We need to continue telling the stories from the Old Testament. Such accounts as those of Adam and Eve, Noah, Jacob, and the sage of the Exodus all have a great bearing on our faith heritage, and we need to know them and retell them.

Faith followers of Jesus will tell the good news and live it out in their lives. Perhaps the most effective teaching and proclamation is not what we say but what we do. At times, going the second mile, being willing to help or just to listen can be the most powerful witness to God's love. Often, it is God's love in action.

A new commandment

On the Thursday before his death, Jesus said to his disciples, "I give you a new commandment, that you love one another. Just as I have loved you, you also should love one another. By this everyone will know that you are my disciples, if you have love for one another" (JOHN 13:34-35).

There are some who have trouble with "commandment language." They think that the gospel cannot be put in the imperative. In a sense, they are correct, but one of the perennial questions is, "What do I do after I say 'I believe'?" Some have answered with a single word: *stewardship*. Stewardship is loving one another. Loving one another is what Jesus asked of his disciples. It is what faithful followers of Jesus do.

John wrote in his first letter: "Beloved, let us love one another, because love is from God; everyone who loves is born of God and knows God. Whoever does not love does not know God, for God is love. God's love was revealed among us in this way: God sent his only Son into the world so that we might live through him. In this is love, not that we loved God but that he loved us and sent his Son to be the atoning sacrifice for our sins. Beloved, since God loved us so much, we also ought to love one another. No one has ever seen God; if we love one another, God lives in us, and his love is perfected in us" (1 JOHN 4:7-12).

Judgment—a lesson in ministry

On one occasion, Jesus presented a word picture of judgment. He described how the Son of Man would come in glory with all his angels, to sit on his throne. All the nations would be gathered before him. As a shepherd separates sheep and goats, the Son of Man would put the sheep to his right and the goats to the left. "Then the king," says Jesus, speaking of himself, "will say to those at his right hand, 'Come, you that are blessed by my Father, inherit the kingdom prepared for you from the foundation of the world; for I was hungry and you gave me food, I was thirsty and you gave me something to drink, I was a stranger and you welcomed me, I was naked and you gave me clothing, I was sick and you took care of me, I was in prison and you visited me.' Then the righteous will answer him, 'Lord, when was it that we saw you hungry and gave you food, or thirsty and gave you something to drink? And when was it we saw you a stranger and welcomed you, or naked and gave you clothing? And when was it that we saw you sick or in prison and visited you?' And the king will answer them, 'Truly I tell you, just as you did it to one of the least of these who are members of my family, you did it to me'" (MATTHEW 25:34-40).

This description of judgment is of great value to stewards who wish to know what their mission and ministry should be. It is not a surprising description. Jewish religion had long said that such things should be done. Perhaps the classic statement was that of Micah: "What does the Lord require of you but to do justice, and to love kindness, and to walk humbly with your God?" (MICAH 6:8). Jesus, however, brings a new perspective when he says that when others are helped, it is as if the service were given to God. James will later prescribe: "Religion that is pure and undefiled before God the Father is this: to care for orphans and widows in their distress, and to keep oneself unstained by the world" (JAMES 1:27).

What stewards do

As faithful followers of Jesus we are called to live our lives in obedience to the commands of Christ. We are called to minister and witness in his name: to feed the hungry, give drink to the thirsty, to practice hospitality, to clothe the naked, to tend to the sick, to help those who are not free, to be a blessing to others because God has blessed us. But we do not do these things alone. Our Lord goes with us. His promise to be with us to the end of the age is itself an eternal promise. And we do not do these things with our own strength, as we shall see in the light of Pentecost.

QUESTIONS FOR REFLECTION

1. We have been called to go, teach, baptize and make disciples. What are some of the opportunities at this time to do these things?

2. How should we teach and tell the good news of Jesus?

3. To be faithful we should live in obedience to the commands of Christ. What does this mean and how do we do it?

13

CALLED TO BE
FAITHFUL STEWARDS

The Holy Spirit empowers us

Luke begins his second volume, the Acts of the Apostles, with a brief review of his gospel account, much as the producers of mini-series summarize previous episodes for their television audience.

"In the first book, Theophilus, I wrote about all that Jesus did and taught from the beginning until the day when he was taken up to heaven, after giving instructions through the Holy Spirit to the apostles whom he had chosen. After his suffering he presented himself alive to them by many convincing proofs, appearing to them during forty days and speaking about the kingdom of God. While staying with them, he ordered them not to leave Jerusalem, but to wait there for the promise of the Father. 'This,' he said, 'is what you have heard from me; for John baptized with water, but you will be baptized with the Holy Spirit not many days from now'" (Acts 1:1-5).

What is the will of God—and how do you do it?

The disciples were trying to put everything into perspective in an attempt to understand what was happening. Peter had confessed that Jesus was the Messiah, the Son of God. The disciples knew this. And they knew that Jesus had died and been raised again by God. Was this, then, the time when Jesus would restore the kingdom to Israel? It was the age-old question, couched in human, political terms. Perhaps the disciples still did not understand fully, but would when the Holy Spirit came upon them. For the time being, Jesus seemed to ignore the way in which the question was asked, and replied: "It is not for you to know the times or periods that the Father has set by his own authority. But you will receive power when the Holy Spirit has come upon you; and you will be my witnesses in Jerusalem, in all Judea and Samaria, and to all the ends of the earth" (ACTS 1:7-8).

The birthday of the church

The disciples had come together for Pentecost. It was one of three major Jewish festivals for which it was expected that all who could, would come to Jerusalem. The other two were Passover and the Feast of the Tabernacles. All three, in one way or another, celebrated great events in the life of Israel, and were important agricultural holidays as well. Each lasted eight days. On Pentecost the Israelites celebrated the wheat harvest, the first harvest of grapes and other fruit, and the giving of the Law to Moses on Mount Sinai.

Pilgrims from Palestine and throughout the ancient world made the journey to Jerusalem. For some it was the trip of a lifetime, the only time they would ever be in their holy city.

"Suddenly from heaven," says Luke, "there came a sound like the rush of a violent wind, and it filled the entire house where [the disciples] were sitting. Divided tongues, as of fire, appeared among them, and a tongue rested on each of them. All of them were filled with the Holy Spirit and began to speak in other languages, as the Spirit gave them ability" (ACTS 2:2-4).

Peter's sermon

Jerusalem was filled with people "from every nation under heaven" (ACTS 2:5). When they heard the sound of the violent wind, they rushed to see what was happening. They could scarcely believe their ears and eyes. Here were the disciples, all Galileans—everyone could see that—but they were speaking languages that could be understood by Parthians, Medes, Elamites, and members of every other nationality represented. How could this be? An even better question: "What does this mean?" (ACTS 2:12). Some in the crowd had an answer: "They are filled with new wine" (ACTS 2:13).

That was too much for Peter. Addressing the crowd, he said: "It is only nine o'clock in the morning. These men are not drunk. What you see here is the fulfillment of what was spoken by the prophet Joel: 'In the last days God declares, I will pour out my Spirit upon all flesh, and your sons and daughters shall prophesy, and your young men shall see visions, and your old men shall dream dreams'" (see ACTS 2:14-17). Then Peter launched into an eloquent sermon in which he told the story of Jesus, how he lived, died, and was brought back to life. "This Jesus God raised up," said Peter to those who were Israelites, "and of that all of [the disciples of Jesus] are witnesses. Being therefore exalted at the right hand of God, and having received from the Father the promise of the Holy Spirit, he has poured out this that you both see and hear . . . Therefore let the entire house of Israel know with certainty that God has made him both Lord and Messiah, this Jesus whom you crucified" (ACTS 2:32-33, 36).

Luke tells us that those listening to Peter were so moved by his sermon that they said to him and the other disciples: "Brothers, what should we do?" Peter replied: "Repent and be baptized every one of you in the name of Jesus Christ so that your sins may be forgiven" (ACTS 2:37-38). So we come full cycle. This was the message John the Baptist preached before the ministry of Jesus; and now, in the light of the life, death, resurrection and ascension of Jesus, it became the message of the early church. "Repent and be baptized!"

Peter told his listeners that they would receive the Holy Spirit; that the promise was for them, their children, and all who respond. On that day, some three thousand people were baptized. Luke sums up the result:

> Awe came upon everyone, because many wonders and
> signs were being done by the apostles. All who

believed were together and had all things in common;
they would sell their possessions and goods and
distribute the proceeds to all, as any had need. Day by
day, as they spent much time together in the temple,
they broke bread at home and ate their food with glad
and generous hearts, praising God and having the
goodwill of all the people. And day by day the Lord
added to their number those who were being saved
(ACTS 2:43-47).

From disciples to apostles

Note that they are no longer called *disciples*, but *apostles*. The
change is significant. At first they were learners (disciples).
Now they are persons sent on a mission (apostles). We are the
modern counterparts of Jesus' disciples. We must continue to
study and learn. But we are also the modern counterparts of
the apostles. We are sent with a mission in our time just as
the apostles were sent to be witnesses to the ends of the earth.
We are called, empowered, and sent to witness and serve, to
be faithful stewards of all that God has given us.

Paul, writing to Titus, summarizes the theology underlying
our stewardship response: "When the goodness and loving
kindness of God our Savior appeared, he saved us, not because
of any works of righteousness that we had done, but according
to his mercy, through the water of rebirth and renewal by the
Holy Spirit. This Spirit he poured out on us richly through
Jesus Christ our Savior, so that, having been justified by his
grace, we might become heirs according to the hope of eternal
life" (TITUS 3:4-7).

The task of Christian stewards

It has been said that we live in "the time of the church"—that
in-between time, the time between Christ's ascension and his
coming again. During this time the church is the body of
Christ. During this time we take on the role of suffering servant.
During this time—now—we are called upon to feed his sheep.

After he fed the five thousand, you will remember, Jesus eluded the clutches of those who sought to make him king. Later, when they found him, Jesus said that they were looking for him only because they wanted to be fed again. "Do not," he said to them, "work for the food that perishes, but for the food that endures for eternal life, which the Son of Man will give you" (JOHN 6:27). They asked, "How can we be sure that you are speaking the words of God? What sign are you going to give us? After all, our ancestors ate bread in the wilderness, miraculously provided by Moses." "No," replied Jesus, "it wasn't Moses who gave you that bread; it was God. The true bread of God comes down from heaven and gives life to the world" (see JOHN 6:28-33). "Sir," they pled, "give us this bread always." Jesus answered, "I am the bread of life. Whoever comes to me will never be hungry, and whoever believes in me will never be thirsty" (JOHN 6:34-35).

This, then, is the bread with which the first apostles, and we, the modern apostles, are to feed the sheep. This does not mean, of course, that we merely provide spiritual food and ignore physical bread. Dr. A. D. Mattson was fond of saying, "If a man is hungry, feed his body first; then his soul."

They gave themselves . . .

The early church learned the meaning of stewardship and sharing early in its life. Paul tells about the Macedonians, who in a time of poverty and affliction, gave generously to the collection Paul was making for the Christians in Jerusalem. The Macedonians did more than give according to their means; they gave beyond their means. But most importantly, reports Paul, "they gave themselves first" (see 2 CORINTHIANS 8:1-5). This is still the basic (and best) pattern for Christian stewardship: to give oneself first, and then out of that commitment to manage all the gifts that God has given.

The widow's might

The apostles continued to preach the good news and tell stories from the life of Jesus. Luke tells of a day when Jesus and his disciples were at the temple. Observing the people who put money in the offering box, Jesus pointed out a widow who contributed two copper coins. He said to the disciples, "This poor widow has put in more than all of them; for all of them have contributed out of their abundance, but she out of her poverty has put in all she had to live on" (LUKE 21:3-4). This is often referred to as the story of the widow's mite, because the old English translation used the word *mite,* the smallest coin known, to describe her offering. The story is often used to illustrate the concept of Christian stewardship.

Does it mean that we have not done enough until we have given all we have? Of course not. Rather, it points to motive. The others whom Jesus observed that day gave "out of their abundance," meaning that they were not about to deny themselves. They gave, but it was what they could easily afford. The widow, on the other hand, gave all she had. Thus, she becomes for us a model of unselfishness. It is not the amount of the gift, but the spirit that prompts the giving. That was the widow's strength; or, put another way—her might!

Willing to be a slave

Throughout his ministry, Jesus understood everything he did to be an expression of his role as the suffering servant. Perhaps the word *servant* is not strong enough; *slave* would be better. Paul may have been quoting the words of an early hymn when he wrote that Jesus "did not regard equality with God as something to be exploited, but emptied himself, taking the form of a slave" (PHILIPPIANS 2:6-7).

John tells us that Jesus, during the last supper with his disciples, got up from the table and, removing his outer garment (he was now dressed as a slave would be), got a basin with water and began to wash the feet of the disciples. Peter, as ever the one to speak out of turn, yet always with good intentions, told Jesus: "You will never wash my feet." Peter's heart was in the right place, but he was wrong. "Unless I wash you," says Jesus, "you have no share with me." "Then," said Peter, "don't stop at washing my feet. Wash my hands and my head as well!" (see JOHN 13:3-9).

Luke tells us that during the last supper the disciples got into an argument over which one of them was the greatest. Jesus intervenes. "The kings of the Gentiles lord it over them; and those in authority are called benefactors. But not so with you; rather the greatest among you must become like the youngest, and the leader like one who serves. For who is greater, the one who is at the table or the one who serves? Is it not the one at the table? But I am among you as one who serves" (LUKE 22:25-27).

The model for Christian stewardship is that of the servant. Perhaps Paul put it best in his letter to the Christians at Colossae. Let it serve, also, as a conclusion to this discussion of the call to be faithful stewards.

> As God's chosen ones, holy and beloved, clothe yourselves with compassion, kindness, humility, meekness, and patience. Bear with one another and, if anyone has a complaint against another, forgive each other; just as the Lord has forgiven you, so you also must forgive. Above all, clothe yourselves with love, which binds everything together in perfect harmony. And let the peace of Christ rule in your hearts, to which indeed you were called in the one body. And be thankful. Let the word of Christ dwell richly; teach and admonish one another in all wisdom; and with gratitude in your hearts sing psalms, hymns, and spiritual songs to God. And whatever you do, in word or deed, do everything in the name of the Lord Jesus, giving thanks to God the Father through him (COLOSSIANS 3:12-17).

QUESTIONS FOR REFLECTION

1. Christian stewards have a mission to learn and serve. What are some of the ways we can do both?

2. The Christians in Macedonia, we are told, "gave themselves

first" before giving their money. What does this mean and how might it affect our stewardship?

3. Jesus shows us a model for service in the extreme; that is, being a slave in order to help others. Would we dare to go that far?